Graham Handley MA PHD

Brodie's notes on John Steinbeck's

The Grapes of Wrath

Pan Books London and Sydney

First published 1977 by Pan Books Ltd
Cavaye Place, London SW10 9PG
6 7 8 9
© Graham Handley 1977
Letters quoted are taken from *Steinbeck: A Life in Letters*
(published by Pan Books)
ISBN 0 330 50067 8
Printed and bound in Great Britain by
Richard Clay (The Chaucer Press) Ltd, Bungay, Suffolk

Contents

Page references in these Notes are to the Pan edition of *The Grapes of
Wrath*, but the book is analysed chapter by chapter, so that the Notes
may be used with any edition of the book

The author and his work

John Steinbeck was born on 27 February 1902 in Salinas, California, the third of four children. His parents owned plenty of land, which, as he was to observe, gave people the idea that they were rich, whereas in fact they were often poor, but 'lords of the land, you know, and really low church mice but proud'. By 1919 he had graduated from high school and begun to attend Stanford University, and during the course of his college career he took a number of jobs. One of these was as a ranch-hand near King City: both the experience and the setting were later to be used with a particular sharpness of focus in *Of Mice and Men*. He also worked as a clerk, served in a haberdashery store and in a café, broke in army remounts for 'officers' gentle behinds', and did night shifts loading and stacking sacks of sugar. But he was passionately interested in reading and early determined to become a writer. In 1924 he published two stories in the Stanford *Spectator*, but there was no overnight success, and his voluminous letters convey the sense of his early struggles and the gradual upward trend of his literary and material fortunes.

He read French, Spanish and Russian classics as well as keeping abreast of significant current literature. From 1926 to 1928, he worked on the West Coast, more particularly in the Lake Tahoe area, doing odd jobs. His first novel, *Cup of Gold*, was published in 1929, and was an account, suitably fictionalized, of the buccaneer Sir Henry Morgan: before reaching print it had been rejected altogether seven times. In 1930 he married Carol Henning, and moved to a cottage at Pacific Grove on the Monterey Peninsula, where they settled; Steinbeck was to return to this home throughout his life. In 1931, he first came into contact with McIntosh and Otis, who were destined to remain his literary agents for the rest of his writing career.

Steinbeck's early stories, set in the Californian valleys he knew so well, were published under the title *The Pastures of Heaven*, in 1932 (his agents, he said, 'palmed off *The Pastures* on somebody'). Meanwhile, his wife began to work in the laboratory of Edward F. Ricketts, marine biologist and philosopher, and much more besides; Ricketts was to become Steinbeck's close friend and collaborator and his thinking and way of life were to exert a great influence upon him. *To a God Unknown* and the first two parts of *The Red Pony* were published in 1933, followed by a short story in 1934, 'The Murder'; and then, in 1935, his first great success, *Tortilla Flat*. His strike novel, *In Dubious Battle*, appeared in 1936. In the same year he began work on the short novel which was to rank as one of his masterpieces, *Of Mice and Men*. It was published in 1937 and successfully dramatized, winning a Drama Critics Award. *The Red Pony*, in three parts, was also issued in that year, the fourth part appearing in 1938, together with *The Long Valley*. In 1939 came the most ambitious venture yet, *The Grapes of Wrath*: this novel, as Walter Allen has pointed out, 'includes within itself a considerable part, however, dramatically or melodramatically heightened, of the experience of a considerable number of Americans during the thirties'. Meanwhile, *Tortilla Flat* was filmed.

Steinbeck was now something of a success, with all the attendant perils accruing to his status – letters, autograph hunters, attacks from farmers and landowners who accused him of being a Communist and a liar, and the adverse publicity of a woman claiming to be pregnant by him. Throughout, he was becomingly modest; he had worked very hard on *The Grapes of Wrath*, and had even advised printing a small edition, since he was convinced that it would not be a success. Much of its language was toned down by his agent Elizabeth

Otis, but Steinbeck refused to compromise on the ending, in which Rose of Sharon gives her breast to the starving man. In his own words, 'I tried to write this book the way lives are being lived not the way books are written.' He gave the manuscript to his wife.

In June 1939 the film rights of *Of Mice and Men* and *The Grapes of Wrath* had been sold, the films of the two books being released in 1939 and 1940 respectively; and it was in the latter year that Steinbeck was awarded the Pulitzer prize for *The Grapes of Wrath*. He had always been interested in human existence in its biological aspects, and in 1941 he set off on a marine biology expedition with Ed Ricketts; the fruits of the trip are to be found in *The Log from the Sea of Cortez* and – almost as a by-product – *The Pearl*.

Meanwhile, his marriage to Carol was breaking up; they were divorced in 1942, and in 1943 he married Gwyndolyn Conger. He had by then completed a novel set in (unspecified) occupied territory, *The Moon is Down*, which was also successfully dramatized. In 1943 Steinbeck went to Europe as war correspondent for the *New York Herald Tribune*. Early in 1944 he saw the film *Lifeboat*, which he had written and which was directed by Alfred Hitchcock; but Steinbeck objected to what he considered distortion in the final version of the script. In the same year another of his great successes, *Cannery Row*, was published. By the beginning of 1945 he had practically finished *The Pearl*, of which he said: 'It's a brutal story but with flashes of beauty I think.' This too was filmed, as was *The Wayward Bus*, which came out in 1947.

In 1948, his close friend Ed Ricketts died, following a car crash; though, as Steinbeck was later to write, so acutely did he feel the loss; 'It wasn't Ed who had died but a large and important part of oneself.' In 1948, too, his second wife decided that she wanted a divorce and, by an irony of Fate, in that same year he was elected to the American Academy of Arts and Letters. In 1949 he met and fell in love with Elaine Scott, who was to become his third wife in 1950. He continued to work on film scripts, and published a novel, *Burning Bright*, which was followed in 1951 by *The Log from the Sea of Cortez*.

East of Eden came out in 1952, while in 1954 Steinbeck lived abroad for some months, acting as correspondent for *Le Figaro*, Paris. *Sweet Thursday* was published in the same year, and a musical was made of it in 1955, while 1957 saw *The Short Reign of Pippin IV* completed. He had always been interested in the Arthurian legends, more particularly the work of Malory, and he travelled to Italy to study material there. *Once There Was a War* was published in 1958, but he returned to his obsession with *Morte D'Arthur*, saying 'If Malory could re-write Chrétien for his time, I can re-write Malory for mine'. Thus he spent most of 1959 in Somerset working on *Morte D'Arthur*. It was a fascinating and, for him, compulsive experience, and he wrote to Robert Bolt, who had found him the cottage, '. . . words are truly people, magic people, having birth, growth and destiny'. In 1960 he travelled throughout America, collecting material for the book which was to be called *Travels With Charley*, and in 1961 his last novel, *The Winter of Our Discontent*, was published. In 1962 Steinbeck was awarded the Nobel Prize for Literature. In 1963 he travelled in Eastern Europe and Russia, and was in Warsaw when President Kennedy was assassinated. His letters to Mrs Kennedy (now Jacqueline Onassis) are moving and wise, and she, in her turn, wrote much later to Elaine Steinbeck, 'His letters say more than a whole book could – I will treasure them all my life.' In 1964 Steinbeck was awarded the Presidential Medal of Freedom, and he closely supported the policies of Kennedy's successor, Lyndon B. Johnson. He saw his second son depart for war service in Vietnam, later going himself as correspondent for *Newsday*. He died in 1968, a man who had always shown a loving care for the simple, often underprivileged and wayward people about whom so much of his work was written. This commentary on *The Grapes of Wrath* will, I hope, reveal his main concerns; but I should like to leave this short account of his career with some words of his own which underline the quintessential humanity and humility of the man. Always the love of Malory and of *Morte D'Arthur* was there; as he wrote to Douglas Fairbanks Jnr, '. . . for at least thirty-five years and maybe longer – I have been submerged in research for the timeless *Morte D'Arthur*'. The pull that he felt was deeply sympathetic and intellectual and, in a curious way, spiritual; I know of no other writer who has seen himself, his role and his achievement with such courageous clarity and self-honesty. Here are his words, from a letter to John Murphy written in 1961:

Nine tenths of a writer's life do not admit of any companion nor friend nor associate. And until one makes peace with the loneliness and accepts it as part of the profession, as celibacy is a part of priesthood, until then there are times of dreadful dread. I am just as terrified of my next book as I was of my first. It doesn't get easier. It gets harder and more heartbreaking and finally, it must be that one must accept the failure which is the end of every writer's life no matter what stir he may have made. In himself he must fail as Launcelot failed – for the Grail is not a cup. It's a promise that skips ahead – it's a carrot on a stick and it never fails to draw us on.

Recommended reading

American Literature Selected and Introduced by Geoffrey Moore (Faber & Faber, 1964).

Tradition and Dream Walter Allen (Phoenix House, 1964, Penguin Books, 1965). This is a very good survey of British and American fiction from the 1920s onwards, and with an interesting section on Steinbeck.

Steinbeck: A Life in Letters Edited by Elaine Steinbeck and Robert Wallsten (Heinemann, 1975). (A must for the Steinbeck enthusiast – more revealing than any biography could be.)

To the student

When you come to this book of notes and commentary you will have read *The Grapes of Wrath* and will be seeking help to understand and appreciate its various qualities. Those qualities are literary ones, but each student can only equip himself for a full appreciation of the text by becoming familiar with the geographical location of the events which Steinbeck describes so fully. A map of the United States of America, together with some tracing paper, will enable you to work out the route taken by the Joads and the nature of the terrain through which they travel. Trace it, and you will have some idea of the immensity of their task – and it might be a good idea to pin the map you have made into your file or exercise book so that you can 'log' the various stages of that journey. Only by thus identifying with Steinbeck's people can you understand their task.

No attempt is made in the following commentary to give locations for each town mentioned, as it is felt that the student of these notes should undertake the exercise I have outlined above; nor have I identified any make of car mentioned in the text. These are facts and, though they form a part of Steinbeck's irony, they are not essential to literary appreciation. But every text invites research: some students will find it rewarding to discover what they can about the automobile empires of the nineteen-thirties: others will dig out material on the political, social, industrial, agricultural state of America during that period. As a general background to the history of the United States, the student cannot do better than look at Alistair Cooke's *America*, published in attractive format by The British Broadcasting Corporation in 1973.

Background and title

'I tried to write this book the way lives are being lived not the way books are written.' Thus Steinbeck wrote to his friend Pascal Covici in January 1939, refusing to alter the ending of *The Grapes of Wrath*. During an intolerable and lengthy rainy season in February 1938, he had visited the camps of migrant workers who had made the trip from the drought areas of Oklahoma and other states in order to try to find work in California. He was seriously disquieted by what he saw, and became morally and politically indignant and active. He had gone into the valleys and fields and seen degradation and starvation; his transforming imagination was to stamp the individuality of the Joads on that stark, undeniable reality. By concentrating on the fictional few, he designated the anguished many; ironically, a prominent magazine had sent him out with a photographer into the stricken areas; but not until after *The Grapes of Wrath* was an unqualified success were the pictures published, with apt quotations from the novel.

Steinbeck's own initial reaction to the suffering he saw is recorded in his letters:

There are about 5,000 families starving to death over there, not just hungry but actually starving. The government is trying to feed them and get medical attention to them with the fascist group of utilities and banks and huge growers sabotaging the thing all along the line and yelling for a balanced budget. In one tent there are twenty people quarantined for smallpox and two of the women are to have babies in that tent this week . . . and see if I can't do something to help knock these murderers on the heads. Do you know what they're afraid of? They think that if these people are allowed to live in camps with proper sanitary facilities, they will organize and that is the bugbear of the large landowner and corporation farmer.

And in other letters he wrote:

The death of children by starvation in our valleys is simply shocking
. . . This is the 19th day of rain . . . we found a boy in jail for a felony
because he stole two old radiators because his mother was starving to
death and in stealing them he broke a little padlock on a shed.

Steinbeck abandoned his vigilante novel and began to write of
his experiences in the camps; by 1 June 1938 he could say that
it was going well, though at first he rationed himself to writing
six pages a day, so conscious was he of the need to let the
themes – and the structure – take full shape. By the end of July
he anticipated having written half of the first draft, and in
September he arrived at a title which fitted in terms of both
symbolic and real application. He wrote, 'I like it because it is
a march and this book is a kind of March – because it is in our
own revolutionary tradition and because in reference to the
book it has a large meaning. And I like it because people know
the Battle Hymn who don't know the Star Spangled Banner.'
  Late in 1938 Steinbeck sent the manuscript of *The Grapes of
Wrath* to his agent Elizabeth Otis, with the uncompromising
instruction that 'The Battle Hymn of the Republic', with
music, should go in 'as a page at the beginning'. He advised
printing a small edition of the novel, since he did not think it
would be a popular success. The title, and the 'Battle Hymn'
(from which he took the words 'grapes of wrath'), haunted
him, and he urged Pascal Covici to print '*all, all, all* the verses
. . . They're all pertinent, and they're all exciting'. Covici
obliged by placing the 'Battle Hymn' on the endpapers of the
first edition of the novel. *The Grapes of Wrath* was a tremendous
success, but farmers and landowners attacked Steinbeck, ac-
cusing him of misrepresentation, of lying, of being a Communist: he hated the 'hysteria' of it all, but by October 1939 he
slyly noted that the book had dropped to second place on the
best-sellers' list: '. . . and in six months I'll be forgotten'.

The title was particularly well chosen. Julia Ward Howe's moving and inspiring verses were written on the occasion of her visit to Union troops under General McClellan near Washington in December 1861. They were published in the February 1862 issue of the *Atlantic Monthly*, and immediately became widely popular with Union sympathizers. It was largely because of this that she became the first woman to be elected to the American Academy of Arts and Letters. Thus Steinbeck had the range of association he wanted in the title; for just as the American civil war had been fought over the issue of freedom for the slaves and the preservation of liberty and human dignity, so the modern 'march', in clapped-out vehicles, from the dust through the rotten and the rotting to the rain, should have an extended prose hymn to dignify the deprived and the starving, the modern 'slaves' of circumstance.

One understands, too, why Steinbeck wanted all the verses included. The beautiful words, with their ringing spiritual elevation, are an expression of an abiding religious fervour as distinct from the fits and the 'speaking in tongues' of the hot-gospellers on the one hand and the sordid materialism of man on the other. To print the hymn in its entirety was to call his readers towards the practical Christianity of redressing the wrongs of their fellow men. Just as in nineteenth-century fiction, writers from Scott to George Eliot included chapter epigraphs or mottoes as commentary on their characters' situations, so the inclusion of these verses as epigraph to the whole novel directed readers' attention to an appalling contemporary situation. The title is taken from verse one, but verse two refers to the 'hundred circling camps', while the 'evening dews and damps' are experienced by the migrants, who live largely by the light of 'din and flaring lamps' in camp and roadside. One could, I think, take each verse of the hymn and demonstrate its application to Steinbeck's novel and the sincerity of his theme, and the interested student may care to do so. Perhaps the most important words are 'let us die to make men free', for Casy dies so that his fellows may be free from brutality, starvation, coercion, death. Here is Steinbeck at his most sincere; but, alas, man is too insular, too self-interested, too concerned with his own material prosperity to care over-much for the needs of others. *The Grapes of Wrath* remains as a permanent literary OXFAM, bringing home to the individual conscience the plight of the suffering, and leaving that con-science to action or apathy. It is a moving testimony to Stein-beck's love for his fellow creatures.

Plot and structure

While the plot of *The Grapes of Wrath* is straightforward – as will be evident from the chapter summaries later in this study – the structure is complex, the short chapters interacting with the longer ones. The latter are basically concerned with the movements and temporary settlings of the Joad family on their long trek to California. The plot deals exclusively with this family, and the novel proper begins with Tom Joad getting a lift from an inquisitive truck-driver and being set down somewhere near his father's place. He soon meets the ex-preacher, Casy; and the two of them find the Joad homestead deserted. After they have met Muley Graves, who has not fled from the deserted tractored-out land, they press on to Uncle John's small home, where Tom is reunited with his family.

They set off on the long haul to California, but early on the journey Grampa dies and is buried; they have met the Wilsons, and travel with them for a while. There are roadside stops and halts in camps, the chaos of Hooverville, the wire-enclosed and picketed peach-picking camp, the government-organized, civilized, responsible community haven of Weedpatch. Granma, too, dies; Casy gives himself up to avoid Tom's being taken by the law for tripping a deputy; Connie leaves Rose of Sharon; and Noah, the simple elder son, decides to stay put at one of their stops. The family survives on the pittance for peach-picking; Winfield becomes ill; Rose of Sharon needs more milk to feed the baby she is expecting and, worst of all, Tom, having got through the wire, again meets Casy, who is organizing resistance to the unscrupulous bosses. He sees Casy killed with a pick-handle and, incensed, kills the man who did it. Under Ma's direction the family moves on yet again; Tom is smuggled out of the camp and, when they reach the cotton-picking area, hidden in a culvert. The family picks cotton until the terrible rains come (see the section of this book called *Background and Title*). Rose of Sharon loses her baby; and Ma leads the family on foot from the box-cars to higher ground. There, in a barn, they find a boy with a starving man: the man can take no solid food. Ma persuades Rose of Sharon to give her breast to the man.

Thus, the novel ends, with a number of questions left unanswered: will the Joads, and the many thousands like them, survive? Will the bosses win against organized opposition, or will they succeed in crushing it? Will humanity, compassion, government involvement, prevail against self-interest, narrow aggressive attitudes? Will, ultimately, man's inhumanity to man be brought to an end by right thinking, morally conscious people who have the courage to voice their views and promote action? *The Grapes of Wrath* pulls no punches; Joads and Wilsons are typical of the migrants, just as camp proprietors, deputies and American legion men are typical of all those who resented and stigmatized the 'Okies'. That there was a humane and propagandist intention behind the novel is obvious, and non-divine wrath descended on Steinbeck from the farmers and their backers as a result.

Since his method was to build a fictional frame on the basis of fact as he had seen it (see *Background and Title*), Steinbeck so constructs his novel as to make a running width of commentary on actions and attitudes seen in perspective to the movements of the Joad family. Thus Chapter 1 focuses on the dust-bowl, the land that has become sterile and parched, while Chapter 2 describes Tom's journey in the truck and Chapter 3 the trials and tribulations of the land turtle. The structural pattern of the whole novel is succinctly established in these first three chapters: we move from the general to the particular and thence to nature, for the struggles of the land turtle epitomize the struggles of man. The outside threats to the turtle – the sedan car that deliberately misses it; the light truck that flips it like a tiddly-wink; the red ant that gets inside its shell – all these approximate to the unfriendly weather, the exploitation, the opposition of man to man, the power of the banks, the proprietors, the tractoring of homes and land, all of which the 'Okies' suffer. So intent is Steinbeck on this use of parallelism in man and nature that he never allows us to forget it, and a look at the section on *Style* (and, of course, at the text) will reveal how many of the images are drawn from nature to define man's state or to comment on his actions. As in Steinbeck's other books, descriptions of nature abound, and even a change in the light can be seen as symbolizing a change in the fortunes of the Joad family.

In terms of overall balance in emphasis, fourteen chapters out of thirty deal specifically with the Joads, beginning with Tom in Chapter 2. The Joad chapters are much longer than the others, with the exception of the roadside snack-bar chapter. This has its human contrasts: with the poor migrant and his two children; the rough kindness of the truck-drivers and Al and Mae; and those to whom Mae refers as 'shit-heels'. The planning is very careful, as I have indicated in my brief look at the first three chapters, and throughout the narrative Steinbeck has 'perspective' chapters – either in description of the terrain or of the migrants, a used-car lot, rotting fruit in California, or the blanketing nullity of the rain – before returning sharply to the Joads and their movements from adversity to adversity. Frequently the short perspective chapters are written in the vernacular: the monologue of the car salesman; or Mae in dialogue, bridling or sympathetic. The kind of camp represented by Hooverville is described in the chapter before the Joads settle into it, and the community ideal is lauded before the arrival at Weedpatch. Lush but rotting California is described before the Joads pick peaches; the need for cotton-pickers precedes the Joad's arrival and entry into their temporary home in the box-car. All this means that the novel operates on two levels, that of immediate and personal involvement with the Joads, and that of moral, social and political appraisal of the migrants as a whole and the situations in which they find themselves.

There is little doubt that the strength of the novel lies in the portraits of the Joad family, from the realism of Ma, Tom and Casy, to the element of caricature present in Granma and Grampa and, to a certain extent, in the portrayal of Winfield, Ruthie, Al and Noah. But Steinbeck intends the linking chapters to be taken seriously, and thus they have an important function in the structure. The wider range of reference is in the main tradition of English fiction: for example, George Eliot sets *Middlemarch* against a background of political and medical reform, and structurally these elements of the novel are seen against the development of character. Hardy gives *Tess of the D'Urbervilles* the natural rural background of its time, but we are conscious of the onset of machinery that is to change people's lives; strangely, there are direct parallels between Tess's journeys and the migration of the Joads. And just as George Eliot and Hardy use the omniscient convention and speak in the novel in their *own* voices, so Steinbeck does too (see the section on *Style*).

The structure of *The Grapes of Wrath* embraces the present, but there is an insistent linking with the past, so that Tom, Casy, Ma, Muley, Pa, Grampa and Uncle John all reminisce, thinking of a world that has gone. Muley remembers his Pa, gored by a bull; or himself in the hollow, randy as a billy-goat. These simple, instinctive associations are used structurally as a contrast to the modern used-car lot with its inhuman dedication to the profit motive and the replacing of instinctive behaviour by the sophisticated wiles of the swindler. On all levels this pattern of structural contrast is seen. The one-eyed man in the spare-parts lot is like the one-eyed trucks, so to speak, which the migrants are forced to buy. The expensive, casually identified goodies of Mae's snack-bar are seen in contrast to Ma's simple but substantial preparation of food. Pigs, if you like, are salted, not hamburgered; and into these structural areas Steinbeck injects his own voice, always compassionate, sometimes strident in appeal and denunciation of what is evil and wrong. If we read Joyce or Virginia Woolf, for example, we are made quickly aware that the convention of the author's using his own voice has given way to a determined anonymity, with the consciousness or subconsciousness of character being probed by way of revelation; but Steinbeck does not observe this modern practice and his voice, radical and freedom-loving, is constantly to be found, particularly in what I have called the perspective chapters of *The Grapes of Wrath*. He uses the established tradition of nineteenth-century fiction in a particularly modern way, the way of commitment.

The structure of the novel is thus balanced between the author's appraisal of a situation and his reaction to it, and the creation of authentic characters to demonstrate, in human terms, the appalling nature of that situation. It has to be said that the extended device is not altogether successful, that we prefer the Joads to the eulogy of Manself, accounts of the owner-men, Highway 66 and a list of towns. None the less, such is Steinbeck's narrative sweep that we are carried along by the force of the writing – just as the Joads are carried along with the thousands of others, by the force of adversity. The structure of the novel is interesting in terms of intention and commitment; aesthetically it leaves us a little dissatisfied, as any overt propaganda must. But the form never makes for dullness, and it is filled out by the compassion and humanity of the writer.

Style

Because of the structure of the novel, Steinbeck employs a variety of styles. The first, the major facet of his writing in this novel, is the use of the Okies' vernacular; and that speech, despite the sombreness of their situation, is imbued with humour. This humour is of the earth earthy, like the people; but in any critical appraisal of *The Grapes of Wrath* this facet of Steinbeck's art must be stressed, since it underlines the essential realism of his characterization. A good example of genuine humour – and nearly always it has the nostalgia of the secure past, of reminiscence – is when Tom tells Casy of how Albert Rance, having taken his family to Oklahoma City one Christmas, returns to find that his neighbours have removed all his furniture and fittings: they thought he had left for good. As Tom says, 'Took Albert two weeks drivin' aroun' the neighbours 'fore he got his stuff back.' (p.48)

Frequently the humour is sexual, as one would expect: the kind of harmless dirty story which provokes an appreciative response, as when Tom tells Casy of Willy Feely, who is bashful, taking his heifer over to be mated by the Graves's bull. Elsie Graves and Willy sit on the fence to watch and Elsie, forward and pert and realizing that Willy is sexually aroused, jokes coarsely but cleverly at his expense (p.76). Steinbeck has a marvellous ear for the realities of speech ('somepin jus' bust in her. Ap-appendick or somepin.'), and what he succeeds in doing is to capture the racy and the repetitive in economic innuendo. Thus there is Granma's terrible war-cry: 'Pu-raise Gawd for vittory', and Grampa's unequivocal indelicacy of describing himself as 'full a' piss an' vinegar'. Both are humorous in the manner of a caricature, establishing positive traits with a Dickensian vividness.

But it is not only the Okies who are seen in this way. Monologue or dialogue involving the more sophisticated characters is equally authentic in tone and delivery; as we find when the used-car salesman keeps up all the patter of his trade almost as if he, too, is running – like his vehicles – on verbal gas:

Ther's a dumb bunny looking' at that Chrysler. Find out if he got any jack in his jeans. Some of these farm boys is sneaky. Soften 'em up an' roll 'em into me, Joe. You're doin' good. (p.71)

The contrast with the Okies' speech is obvious, and this contrast is further enhanced by another remove of sophistication in the snack-bar chapter, where Mae appreciates a truck-driver's parody of a popular song: 'you might have been a haddock but you never was a whore'. The religious heritage of the Joads and their like is also given a considered stress, first through Casy, whose delivery remains, though his thought has been transfigured by contemplation and life experience:

'Night-time I'd lay on my back an' look up at the stars; morning I'd set an' watch the sun come up; midday I'd look out from a hill at the rollin' dry country; evenin' I'd foller the sun down. Sometimes I'd pray like I always done. On'y I couldn' figure what I was prayin' to or for. There was the hills, an' there was me, an' we wasn't separate no more. We was one thing. An' that one thing was holy.' (p.88)

Once again, the links between man and nature are apparent. But there is another kind of religion, perhaps best typified by the woman who harangues Rose of Sharon in the Weedpatch camp:

'Gettin' so's you can almos' count the deep-down lamb-blood folks on your toes. An' don' you think them sinners is puttin' nothin' over on God, neither. No, sir, he's a-chalkin' 'em up sin by sin, an' he's drawin' his line an' addin' 'em up sin by sin. God's a-watchin', an' I'm a-watchin'. He's awready smoked two of 'em out.' (p.328)

One could go on giving examples of Steinbeck's superb ability to capture the actuality of speech without parodying it.

This quality of authenticity is heightened by a fine descriptive ability when it comes to physical characteristics. Here is our first sight of Grampa:

His was a lean excitable face with little bright eyes as evil as a frantic child's eyes. A cantankerous, complaining, mischievous, laughing face. He fought and argued, told dirty stories. He was as lecherous as always. Vicious and cruel and impatient, like a frantic child, and the whole structure overlaid with amusement. (p.84)

Here it is the vividness and the economy that arrests our attention, as well as the quality of compassion which informs all Steinbeck's writing. This physical description is extended by the author to encompass understanding of his characters and the way they are. Just after this evocative description of Grampa there is a tellingly muted appraisal of Noah, the eldest son:

there was a listlessness in him toward things people wanted and needed. He lived in a strange silent house and looked out of it through calm eyes. He was a stranger to all the world, but he was not lonely. (p.86)

These last two quotations – again contrasting with each other – reveal Steinbeck's range, and when he comes to describe Ma he lingers with loving care:

She seemed to know that if she swayed the family shook, and if she ever really deeply wavered or despaired the family would fall, the family will to function would be gone. (p.81)

This power to describe the inner as well as the outer person is perhaps most poignantly seen in Rose of Sharon's reaction as she feeds the dying man at the very end of the novel:

Her hand moved behind his head and supported it. Her fingers moved gently in his hair. She looked up and across the barn, and her lips came together and smiled mysteriously. (p.480)

Rose of Sharon has lost her baby and yet, in a curious and individual way, she now possesses one; for the young and the old, equally helpless, need care and love, and her action expresses a love which transcends convention. Here the meek have inherited the earth and, perhaps, the Kingdom of Heaven.

Always in Steinbeck there is a minute account of nature and at the same time a large canvas on which to paint, so that one is made aware of 'each green bayonet' of corn, and of distance, light, and the mystical associations that link man and nature:

The stars went out, few by few, toward the west. And still the family stood about like dream-walkers, their eyes focused panoramically, seeing no detail, but the whole dawn, the whole land, the whole texture of the country at once. (pp.121–2)

Man is irrevocably bound to the earth and to the seasons, and a succession of images establishes the permanent kinship between the small and the large and all-powerful. Nature is variously personified ('the wind cried and whimpered over the fallen corn'), while the life-giving force, the sun, is simply 'as red as ripe new blood'. Tom's fingers and nails are 'as thick and ridged as little clam shells', leaves are 'tattered and scraggly as a moulting chicken', and Casy has 'a neck as stringy and muscular as a celery stalk'. As you read on in the novel, you will find that these examples are multiplied a hundredfold; this is, so to speak, the sympathetic and unifying imagery of *The Grapes of Wrath*. But the machinery that destroys life and changes the course of nature is spoken of in rather a different way. The language is vivid and strongly sexual, but it is sexuality without sex:

Behind the tractor rolled the shining disks, cutting the earth with blades – not ploughing but surgery . . . the harrows combing with iron teeth . . . the long seeders – twelve curbed iron penes erected in the foundry, orgasms set by gears, raping methodically, raping without passion. (p.41)

Thus the parallels between man and machine are expressed, and throughout *The Grapes of Wrath* this parallelism is maintained. Deprived children eat fried dough; the tractor driver eats 'a piece of pie branded like an engine part'. Thus the imagery reflects the man who has become a machine. Chapter 7 in its entirety provides a good example of Steinbeck's method: lists of cars or the parts of cars punctuate the salesman's monologue; the emphasis is on fact, man-created fact as distinct from the natural inheritance of the earth, whether it be dust or peaches or sparse crops. The language of the salesman is a new language, but it is a language which is death to individuality; there is a frightening uniformity about the used cars, for they are rotten through the usage of man just as, later, the Californian fruit is rotten through his abusage.

We have seen that *The Grapes of Wrath* is steeped in images from nature and images from man-made associations, but there is, in addition, a tone, heard often in the narrative, which is at once elevating and disturbing. (It is reminiscent of D. H. Lawrence's tone in *The Rainbow*; in dealing with the generations of the Brangwens as the generations of man – and always keeping his title in mind – Lawrence uses a biblical tone that gives his narrative a universality.) Steinbeck uses a similar device: sometimes it consists of simple repetition ('And the migrants streamed in on the highways and their hunger was in their eyes, and their need was in their eyes'); at other times the style reflects a religion of humanity, a belief in individuality and the simple, abiding needs of man:

The last clear definite function of man – muscles aching to work, minds aching to create beyond the single need – this is man. To build a wall, to build a house, a dam, and in the wall and house and dam to put something of Manself, and to Manself take back something of the wall, the house, the dam; to take hard muscles from the lifting, to take the clear lines and form from conceiving. For man, unlike anything organic or inorganic in the universe, grows beyond his work, walks up the stairs of his concepts, emerges ahead of his accomplishments. . . . Having stepped forward, he may slip back, but only half a step, never the full step back. This you may say and know it and know it. (p.160)

This kind of style is admittedly propagandist, but Steinbeck is a committed writer, and what he is trying to do by explaining his beliefs in this way is to elevate and dignify people like the Joads, people whose simple aspirations are denied by a society bent on profit at the expense of humanity. This elevation, this looking beyond the immediate to establish a permanent principle in life, invests *The Grapes of Wrath* with a certain timelessness. This is confirmed by the ending of the novel; the struggle for survival goes on and on and on.

I have deliberately kept this section on *Style* short, merely providing a few examples to guide students towards a fuller appreciation of Steinbeck's art: as you read the novel, various aspects of a writer's modes of expression become clearer to you, and in a long novel like this there are doubtless facts which have not been mentioned in this introduction. What I want to stress is Steinbeck's superb ear for realistic dialogue, using the vernacular of the Okies, individualized according to character; his ability to capture the insistent monologue of the salesman, and the monologue and dialogue at one remove, that of the owner men and the tenants in linking chapters. The novel is rich in natural description, and this in turn is underlined by a permanent pattern of imagery, which reflects the identity and relationship of man and nature and the effects of the advent of machinery. The authorial tone, built on a structure of deliberate repetition (and life is repetitive too) helps to unify the novel and universalize its themes. Steinbeck is the great creator of atmosphere, whether it be the sterility of dust, the suddenness of violence (witness the killing of Casy) or the vivid reminiscence which is immediate and felt by character and reader alike. His memory for natural and local anecdote gives the text a richly satisfying fullness and continuity, and Chapter 9, where we have a monologue from the consciousness of a tenant, is a good example of this. Steinbeck's style can be impassioned in denunciation, and it can damn by simple statement:

Frantic men pounded on the doors of the doctors; and the doctors were busy. And sad men left word at country stores for the coroner to send a car. The coroners were not too busy. The coroners' wagons backed up through the mud and took out the dead . . . At night the frantic men walked boldly to hen roosts and carried off the squawking chickens. If they were shot at, they did not run, but splashed sullenly away; and if they were hit, they sank tiredly in the mud. (p.459)

There are moments of poetry, but there are many more moments of pathos; the humour, whether coarse, nostalgic, sexual, underlines the resilience of the human spirit in adversity, and sustains the realism of the narrative.

The characters

Ma

Her full face was not soft; it was controlled, kindly. Her hazel eyes seemed to have experienced all possible tragedy and to have mounted pain and suffering like steps into a high calm and a superhuman understanding. She seemed to know, to accept, to welcome her position, the citadel of the family, the strong place that could not be taken . . . She moved toward him lithely, soundlessly in her bare feet, and her face was full of wonder . . . And then her fingers went up to his cheek as a blind man's fingers might. And her joy was nearly like sorrow.

Almost from the beginning we follow the fortunes and misfortunes of Tom Joad, but Ma is the most impressive, sympathetic and subtly explored character in *The Grapes of Wrath*. She succours and saves the family, takes adversity with resolution and courage, makes decisions when they have to be made, is warm, kind, resilient and forthright when the need arises. In a world where the men nominally rule and the women prepare their food and maintain the essential creature comforts, Ma rules in fact, her integrity and permanence being the pivots of the family life. It is part of Steinbeck's art, indeed an integral part, that although Ma seems initially idealized, she grows under his pen into a convincing character, a character rarely able to reveal her emotions yet making us aware of her worry and suffering by the very nature of her imposed control. The return of Tom is a case in point, for after her immediate and spontaneous 'wonder' at his reappearance, she plunges herself into the domestic preparations – as a means of covering the temporary revelation of her deep feelings for the son who has been lost to them for so long. Her humanity, the essential rightness of her thinking, is always stressed; her main concern when she sees Tom is to discover whether he is 'poisoned mad', and she sighs 'Thank God!' when she realizes that he is heart-whole, neither twisted nor bitter after his experiences in McAlester.

Ma is strong and practical, with an earthy pride in her everyday work, constrained though it is by cramped conditions and the perpetual moving on; she is apprehensive about the trip to California, wondering if what the handbills say is true, but beneath her methodical day-to-day attention to the chores there is a sense of humour, as we see when she says that peach-picking would be nice, and that 'maybe you could snitch a little ratty one sometimes'. She treats Grampa like the naughty child that he often is, telling him 'They don't let people run aroun' with their clothes unbutton' in California.' She thoroughly respects Casy, and identifies herself immediately with his simple creed: 'Gonna cuss an' swear an' hear the poetry of folks talkin' ' – with the simple word 'Amen'. She is an indefatigable worker, working with her son Noah at the carcasses of the pigs in order to salt them down and provide food for the journey. But when Casy suggests that she is 'sick-tar'd', she straightens her shoulders and makes the decision to part with some of the things she has treasured: photographs, letters; in other words, memories. She puts nearly all of them into a box:

Then gently and tenderly she closed the box and smoothed the top carefully with her fingers. Her lips parted. And then she stood up, took her lantern, and went back into the kitchen. She lifted the stove lid and laid the box gently among the coals. (p.117)

The action symbolizes her capacity for sacrifice, a determination to face up to the challenge of the new life despite the emotional draw of the old.

Ma's responsibilities accumulate, and always she acts: she doses Grampa with soothing-syrup when he proves recalcitrant about going; when they finally do set off she tries to look back

but cannot, though we are told that there was 'a great weari-
ness in her eyes'. Again, this underlines her silent feeling, a
feeling unvoiced for the most part throughout the action. Her
concern is for the others: for the condition of Grampa and
Granma; how Rose of Sharon is feeling; whether it is safe for
Tom to cross the boundary line. All these absorb her thoughts
but are in abeyance once the cooking and washing demand
her energy. It is when they meet the Wilsons that the fine
gentleness of Ma's nature is seen; Grampa dies in Sairy's tent,
and Ma lays him out – 'in pity she tore a strip from her own
apron and tied up his jaw' – afterwards showing her thoughtfulness for Granma by getting Rose of Sharon to lie down with
her, and later saying to the painfully-ailing Sairy, 'We gonna
see you get through.'

Her sense of the family as a unit is uppermost, and she is
worried when Rose of Sharon tells her that she and Connie are
going to live in a town and that Connie is going to study; Ma's
family creed is summed up in her own words, 'It ain't good for
folks to break up.' She adheres to this strictly, and finds herself
in opposition to all the men when the truck breaks down and
they suggest splitting up temporarily. She seizes the jack
handle, refuses to go, and tells Pa: 'I'll light into you. An' you
ain't so sure you can whup me anyways . . . I'll wait till you got
your back turned, or you're setting down, an' I'll knock you
belly-up with a bucket.' (p.179)

From now on it is crisis upon crisis for Ma. Granma is ill;
Rose of Sharon is worried about her baby; and Tom has to tell
her that Noah is not going on with them. When they stop by
the roadside for a temporary camp, Ma has to cope with the
biliously religious woman who wants to hold a prayer meeting
for Granma. Here she first hears the derogatory term 'Okies',
and responds with the simple dignity of her nature. Then the
severity of Sairy Wilson's illness is brought home to her: there
is a deep, sympathetic bond between the two women. When

Ma has spent ten minutes in the Wilson tent, she returns to where the men are talking. Wilson refuses to take money from them for food, but Ma is adamant:

Ma took the two bills from Pa's hand. She folded them neatly and put them on the ground and placed the pork pan over them. 'That's where they'll be,' she said. 'If you don' get 'em, somebody else will.' (p.234)

When they push on yet again, and the truck is stopped for an 'Agricultural inspection', Ma 'hoisted herself with huge strength' to show the officer Granma's state (in reality she is dead). This exertion of her body and willpower drains Ma of strength; once again she has held on, this time without the family's knowing, so that Granma 'can get buried in a nice green place'. Casy pays her the tribute we all feel when he says, 'John, there's a woman so great with love – she scares me. Makes me afraid an' mean.' But money is very short, and Granma has to have a country burial. Ma adjusts to the experiences of Hooverville splendidly, but her inherent kindness, shown when she feeds some of the poorer children, gets her into trouble with one of the jealous and deprived residents. She does her best to keep Rose of Sharon occupied when Connie disappears, and is tender of the girl's feelings when the men criticize Connie.

After Casy's arrest Ma is even more concerned on Tom's account, her fear always being that 'The family's breakin' up.' So intent is she on avoiding trouble on her son's behalf that she keeps a tight grip on Tom when men wearing American Legion caps stop the truck. Her love for Tom is very great; when they reach the government camp she becomes 'girlish' when she is talking to him, and her intense pride in herself – after all the privations and suffering she has experienced – is reflected in her 'brushing water through her hair', though there is a delicious humour in the fact that she is doing this in

the men's toilet. Her delight in the new, unfamiliarly comfort-
able conditions is tempered by a moving and human response
when she, who is so used to giving, now receives consideration
and kindness unasked. When the manager has come to visit,
and she hears him speaking warmly to other people, we are
told that she 'put down her head and she fought with a desire
to cry'. But she doesn't, for soon the family appear and her
emotionalism is lost in the needs of Uncle John (recovering
from his drunkenness the night before) and the children.

Again, Ma has to rally herself to lift the waning morale of
Rose of Sharon, who has been interrogated by a trouble-
making religious lady, and then she has to receive the Ladies'
Committee. This is an ordeal, since Ma, who is nothing if not
respectable, has great pride in herself and her family despite
their poverty; that pride is sorely tested when Mrs Sandry,
who had upset Rose of Sharon, appears and asks her if she has
been 'saved'. Ma, forthright and uncompromising, is defend-
ing her young, and reduces Mrs Sandry to a fit. As she says to
the manager:

'If she comes back, I might hit her. I ain't sure. I won't let her worry
my girl no more.' (p.341)

Ma's optimism and faith in an ultimately good destiny helps to
sustain Rose of Sharon; but there is no work available, and
once again – this time because she is worried about Winfield as
well as Rose of Sharon – she suggests that they move on. She
finds Rose of Sharon eating slack lime, and remembers the time
when she ate coal herself. In order to raise the girl's spirits she
pierces her ears so that she will be able to wear ear-rings, a
subtle way of flattering her vanity and rekindling her pride in
herself. Once again, she organizes their departure in the early
hours, confiding to Tom that she gets 'panicky' sometimes.
Her next experience is the overcharging at the Hooper store,
and after her exchange with the storekeeper over 'a dirty thing

like this' she voices the creed which, together with her belief in the family, characterizes her way of life:

'I'm learnin' one thing good,' she said. 'Learnin' it all a time, ever' day. If you're in trouble or hurt or need – go to poor people. They're the only ones that'll help – the only ones.' (p.398)

Ma believes in destiny, not in the simple sense that she and her family will survive, but also in her appraisal of Tom and his fate. Consequently when Tom kills Casy's murderer she is prepared, and after the initial shock of the news she organizes the family into covering up for him. She realizes that once more they have to move, this time to take Tom beyond the reach of the searchers. Again, the need for the family to stick together is foremost in her mind; they make for the box-cars of the cotton pickers, Ma memorizing the culvert where Tom is to hide so that she can care for him.

The final phase of the novel shows Ma practical and decisive as ever, making their part of the box-car a home; she ensures that all of them – and Rose of Sharon in particular – have good food. But Ruthie's mention of Tom to another child provokes yet another crisis. Ma, focus always of unvoiced love, receives from Ruthie, whom she has comforted by her words, the tribute of demonstration:

Ruthie's body hurtled across the car. She grabbed Ma around the middle and buried her head in Ma's stomach, and her strangled sobs shook her whole body. Ma tried to loosen her, but the grubby fingers clung tight. Ma brushed the hair on the back of her head gently, and she patted her shoulders. 'Hush,' she said. 'You didn' know.' (p.438)

Ma's leave-taking of Tom is one of the most moving sequences in the novel, mainly because once again we see the anguish beneath the controlled exterior; arrived back at the car, she exerts herself to keep Al, who wants to get married to Aggie Wainwright, within the family fold until Spring. Next morning, she urges the men out to pick, herself going with them.

Then the rain arrives, and with it the Rose of Sharon's still-born child. Again Ma takes the decision, moving on up the road to higher land, and eventually reaching the barn where they find the starving man. Then Ma wordlessly indicates to Rose of Sharon what she must do, as 'the two women looked deep into each other'. And Rose of Sharon gives her breast to the man.

Thus the novel ends as Ma has lived; her life has been devoted to others, more particularly her family, but she is the true Christian as against those who hold meetings with ecstasy and 'sperits'. Courageous, spirited, self-denying; setting her worries aside for the needs of others; virtually unlettered; loving, practical, resilient; fiercely sentimental and possessive: she represents inherent goodness of nature; and as such she is an optimistic affirmation of Steinbeck's transcendent faith in the capacity and stamina of the human spirit in the face of adversity.

Tom

'I been thinkin' how it was in that gov'ment camp, how our folks took care a theirselves, an' if they was a fight they fixed it theirself; an' they wasn't no cops wagglin' their guns, but they was better order than them cops ever give. I been a-wonderin' why we can't do that all over. Throw out the cops that ain't our people. All work together for our own thing – all farm our own lan'.'

Tom Joad is the central character in *The Grapes of Wrath*, and in a sense his journey back to the family and with them to California is paralleled by the larger journeys of the migrants themselves. He comes through suffering to the kind of awareness implicit in the quotation above; twice he kills, once in the reflex of anger at a dance, and once in the impulse of anger but the cause of justice. Tom is seen in strong contrast with his brothers Noah and Al, and he, like Ma, is a moral centre between their extremes. We first meet him when he gets a lift with the truck driver who noses out his secret; Tom is far from simple and, as he says, 'when you been in stir a little while, you can smell a question comin' from hell to breakfast'. Underneath the exterior he is forced to display, Tom is soft and as attached to the family ideal as Ma; he picks up the turtle as a present for Winfield, whom he hasn't seen for four years. His meeting with Casy is a great, though at the time unknown, influence on his own development. For, as time and tribulation goes on, he comes to see that the preacher's way of thinking is right; moreover he is able to reminisce with Casy, to think back on his youth and early manhood and thus feel integrated once more into the family. Tom is adept at making the best of things, as he did in McAlester: it is not that he is insensitive, but he has a capacity for acceptance, and it will be seen that he is strongly like Ma in many facets of his character.

At first Tom wonders and is shocked that the family have gone, but after hearing Muley's account he accepts this, too, and decides to go after them to Uncle John's. His consideration for others is shown when he surprises his father, but is frightened of scaring his mother by his unexpected return. Tom hates being pushed around, and Ma has to keep a brake on his reactions throughout the journey. He soon demonstrates that his mother's practical ability is his, for his knowledge of trucks complements Al's at every turn of the tortuous journey. His philosophy of life, as he tells Ma, is based on his prison experiences: that every day must be taken as it comes, without fretting about the future. It is a philosophy of which Ma approves, but Tom adds that he has heard there are too many people in California, all wanting work, and that wages are low. Significantly, the family, the men, accept Tom back into their councils: in fact, they do more than that – they turn to him; he has lost none of his practical touch by being in prison, and helps slaughter the pigs efficiently and quickly. It is Tom who suggests that they leave Uncle John's instead of mooning around, and this reflects his own wish to undertake the journey and see what will come of it. It is Tom who points out the seriousness of Grampa's wish to stay, and who helps Ma to take action which will ensure that he accompanies them. Tom has a certain fierceness of authority in him, and at their first stop deals with the petrol attendant in summary fashion by telling him that 'We're payin' our way.' But his insight into the reality of the situation, and a certain compassion, shows through when he says:

'I didn' mean to sound off at ya, mister. It's the heat. You ain't got nothin'. Pretty soon you'll be on the road yourse'f.' (p.136)

He realizes that Ma is concerned that he should not break his parole; but, as he says, 'if I don't do no crimes, they won't give a damn'. He is tactful enough to appeal to the Wilson's sense of hospitality when he wants to camp beside them; and he is compassionate, thoughtful, kind, in suggesting that Joads and Wilsons join up on the journey. He is resilient and tolerant in dialogue with Al about the truck, for he knows that his brother fancies himself as a mechanic; but he comes into conflict with Ma when he suggests that the rest of the family go on while he and Casy fix the truck. Again, that sense of balance, a natural maturity if you like, breaches the gap, and he gives in – on behalf of Pa and the others, without loss of pride or dignity: 'You win, Ma. Put away that jack handle 'fore you hurt somebody.' At no time does Tom show his mother less than complete respect.

Gradually he comes under the influence of Casy's humanitarian creed, which is more fully articulated than his own; but his own feelings, like Ma's, are closely guarded. When Al tells him of Ma's attachment to him (Tom) – 'Kinda crying down inside of her throat' – he pulls his cap 'down low over his eyes'. He has no time for self-pity or self-indulgence, and raps the one-eyed man who looks after the spare-parts junk yard by saying, 'There ain't nothin' the matter with you. Buy yaself some white pants. Ya gettin' drunk and cryin' in ya bed, I bet.' His independence of spirit is seen when they reach the camp and the proprietor refers to him as a bum:

'I'll go for you an' your deputy with my mitts – here now, or jump Jesus. But there ain't no good in it.' (p.199)

When they hear that conditions are bad in California, Tom yanks Pa's arm in order to make him stop talking of it in front of Ma and thus upsetting her hopeful vision. Characteristically, as they leave the camp, he hurls a clod at the proprietor's house. It is an outlet for his frustration, a sign of his contained aggression which has had tragic consequences for him once and which is to get him into trouble again in the future.

When the travellers reach a spot in California, prior to crossing the desert, Noah decides to stay. Tom has the responsibility of telling Ma and, like Ma, he has the sense to see that they must press on. Their experiences in Hooverville make Tom angry, and already the seeds of that rebellion which later grow in Casy are to be found in Tom, too. As he says to the young man, 'I'll kick the hell outa somebody', and when he talks to Casy he sees what the latter sees, that 'They's a army of us without no harness.' He tries to contain Al's feelings of frustration, but with the arrival of the contractor and the protecting deputies and their attempt to take Floyd, Tom's own frustration breaks out. He trips the deputy and unloads his gun (which has shot off a woman's fingers), thus showing once more his capacity for getting into trouble. This time Casy takes the blame, but the Joads now have to move on yet again. Before they do so, Tom displays his sense of responsibility: he goes out to retrieve Uncle John after the latter had drunk two bottles of whisky. The drive to the government camp is fraught with danger when the American legion men stop the truck; Tom, firmly under the guidance of Ma, whines to them, turns the truck but then takes a detour back in the direction they wish to go. He is humiliated and angry and tells Ma, 'I got to get away from 'em. I'm scairt I'll kill one.'

Tom, now the leader of the family in the practical sense, drives to the Weedpatch government camp and gives Ma a lift of morale by telling her how pleasant it is. His natural friendliness establishes a relationship with the Wallaces, and they get him five days' work, which ensures that there is some money coming in for the family. Tom, used to the 'system' of the prison, ironically appreciates the system of the Committee in the camp, and sees for the first time people working together to achieve standards and right behaviour – a communal way of life based on firm morality. But he is beginning to be aware that outside there is an agitation of great strength operating against the 'Okies' and the so-called 'Reds'. When that agitation manifests itself in the threat to break up the Saturday night dance at the camp, Tom is instrumental in detaining the troublemakers who have been sent in. But at the scent of trouble Ma, who is also worried about the state of Winfield and Rose of Sharon, suggests moving on. She wants to go to Maryville, but Tom, who is far-sighted and has heeded all the talk he has heard, would rather head north for the cotton-picking areas. He defers to Ma, and they get through the pickets and arrive at the peach-picking site; Tom later gets outside the fence, meets Casy, and kills the man who has killed the preacher. The fate which Ma so feared for him is upon him, but afterwards he tells Ma that he 'don' feel no worse'n if he killed a skunk'. He hides in the culvert when they reach the box-cars for the cotton-pickers and when Ma comes to see him he has had plenty of time to think; his conclusions represent not only the influence of Casy but the effect of privation, suffering, frustration. Tom has acquired a new awareness, an ideal of communal responsibility which rejects the notion that there must always be underdogs. He is ennobled by its utterance:

'I'll be ever'where – wherever you look. Wherever they's a fight so hungry people can eat, I'll be there. Wherever they's a cop beatin' up a guy, I'll be there. If Casy knowed, why, I'll be in the way guys yell when they're mad an' – I'll be in the way kids laugh when they're hungry an' know supper's ready. An' when our folks eat the stuff they raise an' live in the houses they build – why, I'll be there. (p.444)

Tom is the man who is educated to new responsibilities through suffering, seeing that identification with his fellows is the only way to combat the social and economic evils of his times. He is of the family yet he grows beyond it; as Ma says of him, 'Ever'thing you do is more'n you. When they sent you up to prison I knowed it. You're spoke for.' But whatever his destiny, there is hope as long as there are men like Tom who are prepared to think, examine their consciousness, and act. Again the affirmation is one of positive faith in humanity; Tom has inherited from his mother and acquired through the influence of Casy an abiding concern for others. While the bosses think of red plots, while man abuses man for the sake of the profit motive, while preachers drum up meetings which are outside ordinary human activity, Tom learns to think of the practical solution, where man will work for man and not for himself.

Casy

It was a long head, bony, tight of skin, and set on a neck as stringy and muscular as a celery stalk. His eyeballs were heavy and protruding; the lids stretched to cover them, and the lids were raw and red. His cheeks were brown and shiny and hairless and his mouth full – humorous or sensual. The nose, beaked and hard, stretched the skin so tightly that the bridge showed white. There was no perspiration on the face, nor even on the tall pale forehead. It was an abnormally high forehead, lined with delicate blue veins at the temples.

Casy is one of the most interesting characters in the novel, an ex-preacher ('a Burning Busher') who admits freely to the sins of the flesh during his 'ministry'; as he puts it, 'the more grace a girl got in her, the quicker she wants to go out in the grass'. He is a thoughtful, intelligent, considerate man who grows in moral stature as the action of the novel develops. His thinking has led him to one definite conclusion:

'There ain't no sin and there ain't no virtue. There's just stuff people do. It's all part of the same thing. And some of the things folks do is nice, and some ain't nice, but that's as far as any man got a right to say.' (p.28)

He is lonely, and joins Tom in the journey to Uncle John's to find his parents; he is a great one for reminiscing, and his account of Tom's baptism is vivid and humorous. He is compassionate and understanding when they meet Muley Graves, telling the latter, 'You're lonely – but you ain't touched.' He feels the situation, the flight, acutely, for he has worked out in his own mind that people need a home, roots to cling to; at the same time there is a resurgence of his sense of mission as he realizes that with people on the move he may be able, once again, to get into communities and preach. There is an element of pathos about him, the need to be accepted, to feel wanted again as he was in the past.

Always Casy is thinking, slowly churning over in his mind the events they are passing through and their significance. When they arrive at the Joads he stays considerately in the background until called by the insistence of Granma to give grace; the Christ-like associations which adhere to Casy throughout the novel are very much present here, when he refers to himself as 'you might say like Jesus went into the wilderness to think His way out of a mess of troubles'. His fluency never deserts him, but his grace is more of a revelation of self than of anything else; he is the preacher of common humanity, humility, self-discovery, with an inherent sense of the rightness of things:

'I can't say no grace like I use' ta say. I'm glad of the holiness of breakfast. I'm glad there's love here. That's all.' (p.89)

But the words are more efficacious than any sermon, and from then on Casy is part of the family. His acceptance by them gives him a clarity of vision, of the natural things in life, and of his own part in it; there is a lyrical note to his feelings:

'Gonna learn why the folks walks in the grass, gonna hear 'em talk, gonna hear 'em sing. Gonna listen to kids eatin' mush. Gonna hear husban' an' wife a-poundin' the mattress in the night. Gonna eat with 'em an' learn.' (p.101)

It would be uncritical to pretend that this is completely con-vincing, for Casy is a somewhat idealized character, and one feels that he is his author's mouthpiece for views which, while they are highly laudable and morally right, are sentimental, even romantic in the utterance. But Casy is attached to the family, and in the moment of need, as Grampa dies, he says the Lord's Prayer at Granma's angry behest; later he says his own prayer over the grave, and the emphasis is on the living rather than the dead:

'An' if I was to pray, it'd be for the folks that don' know which way to turn. Grampa here, he got the easy straight. An' now cover 'im up and let 'im get to his work.' (p.154)

Casy is not very practical, though he helps Tom with the truck. Gradually, his thoughts grow round the idea of some sort of action to counteract the suffering, and he believes 'They's gonna come a thing that's gonna change the whole country.' He comforts Sairy Wilson, moves on with the Joads, and comes to revere Ma. Casy's testing time comes with their arrival in Hooverville. The realization that prayer achieves little and that practical action must replace it is borne fully upon him; events move quickly, and he finds himself covering up for Tom, putting himself in a position where he must be arrested. It is the most altruistic action of his life, and in the car he sits proudly: 'On his lips there was a faint smile and on his face a curious look of conquest'.

Casy has made his decision, and when we next see him – picketing outside the peach-picking compound – his thoughts have been translated into militancy, into rebellion on behalf of the migrants. He has been driven to it by what he has seen and experienced, and before he is killed by the deputy he says, 'You fellas don' know what you're doin'. You're helpin' to starve kids.' Like Tom, Casy is the victim of circumstance. His very thoughtfulness drives him into a corner from which there is no escape except into direct involvement. There are times, as I have said above, when he appears so associated with his author's views as to be unconvincing, but in the main his outline is clear and acceptable. He is sensitive and humane, so intent on trying to penetrate the heart of all matters relevant to the migrant situation and his own that he forgoes sleep in order to think, freedom in order to save Tom, pittance wages in order to fight (and die) for others.

Other characters

The three characters already described in detail are the major characters of the novel, and though everyone else is treated sparsely by comparison, Steinbeck has a vividness of conception that brings his people to life very quickly.

Rose of Sharon ('Rosasharn' to her family) is described in her pregnant state, when 'her whole body had become demure and serious', so much so that she makes her husband Connie a little fearful of her – so changed is she from the 'plump, passionate hoyden' he had married. She is extremely impressionable, fearing throughout that any event can affect her

pregnancy and cause her to lose her baby; thus she is superstitious, but when not superstitious, is looking towards the
future: she and Connie will live in a town, and Connie will
study and they will have a house. She treasures her pregnancy
and 'complained of things that didn't really matter'. She and
Connie are all secrets, but still impassioned, and they make
love on the truck while Granma is lying dead beside Ma. Rose
of Sharon is abashed when she learns of Granma's death, and
pathetic when Connie decides to clear out without saying
anything to anyone.

She has little of the character and firmness of Ma, being too
self-centred to be able to look outside herself; she even goes to
Grampa's graveside with reluctance. With Connie gone, she
pulls herself together in bitterness and resentment in response to
Ma's authority, but Ma protects her from the criticism of
Connie which the male members of the family are disposed to
offer. Rose of Sharon shares the natural excitement of the family
when they settle in the Weedpatch camp, being delighted with
the toilet and washing facilities, but she is so impressionable as
to be greatly upset by the religiosity of a woman in the camp
who tells her the story of a 'sinner' having a dead baby. Ma
later routs Mrs Sandry and assures Rose of Sharon that she was
crazy; but the girl is steeped in self-pity.

She breaks down before the camp dance, dependent as ever
on the strength of Ma, and irked by the teasing of Tom. Later
she broods about not having enough milk, and Ma finds her
eating slack lime. Her essentially simple, somewhat vain nature, responds to Ma's giving her some ear-rings and piercing
her ears. But the state of her depression is such that, when Tom
kills the man, she becomes hysterical and shrieks out her
resentment at him in a self-pitying display of temper. Yet she
guards Tom, and ensures that he gets some sleep. Rose of
Sharon, now very large, decides to go out and pick cotton;
later she becomes feverish and, despite the efforts of Ma and

Mrs Wainwright, loses her baby. She 'screamed fiercely under the fierce pains' of labour. The experience of suffering and loss strangely leaves her with some kind of strength, and when, at Ma's suggestion, she bares her breast for the starving man she acquires a kind of mystical maturity and fulfilment. She thus symbolizes the capacity to give, to put the need of another before her own. We recall her one-time daintiness, the careful washing of a tin mug, and note the advance.

Pa and *Uncle John* are rather similar characters: both are guilt-ridden; Pa over his clumsy delivery of Noah which, he believes, has shaped his son's character; and Uncle John over the manner of his wife's death. Pa responds to Tom's return by suggesting that they surprise Ma; but generally speaking he is a pale character compared with Ma, though he does have the initiative to dig and make a bank against the floods. He is unsuccessful, and draws down resentment upon himself.

Uncle John has the merit of eccentricity. He spends his life making up for his guilt by giving presents to the children; but once or twice he breaks out – like the time when 'he went clear to Shawnee and hired three whores in one bed, and snorted and rutted on their unresponsive bodies for an hour'. After the death of Granma he gets drunk and Tom has to go after him. A close student of the text will find more about both men, but they exist more on a caricature level than on a real one.

Al and *Noah* are as different as two young men can be. Noah lives in a private world of his own, is a good worker but rarely communicates, and decides to stay peacefully at one of the stops – they have just lazed in the water – asking Tom to break the news to Ma. Al is rather different: brash, extrovert, a smart-aleck who is always 'tom-cattin' hisself'. Al looks up to Tom because he has killed a man: he is essentially practical – being girl-mad when there is time for it and truck-mad when there is not. He is proud, conceited, a little arrogant, fond of showing off and being the leader of the journey. He succumbs to a girl in the government camp, but when they move on to the cotton-picking area he takes up, apparently seriously, with Aggie Wainwright, and intends to marry her. Once or twice he has to be put in his place by Tom, but he is a good and conscientious mechanic.

The remaining characters are slight but variously vivid. *Connie* lacks the guts to continue the journey, or perhaps he cannot face the responsibilities of fatherhood. In any case, he and Rose of Sharon tend to keep themselves apart and communicate little in the family circle. *Sairy Wilson* comes vividly alive, immediately establishing a sympathetic *rapport* with Ma (and Casy), having Granpa die in her tent, praising Rose of Sharon and bearing her terrible pain in silence. The imminence of Sairy's death – the fact that she will never complete the journey – gives the novel an additional poignancy. *Her husband* is a kindly, good man, impractical but appreciative of the Joads's help, but living in the shadow of his awareness of Sairy's anguish. *Muley Graves* is a little 'touched' (though Casy says he isn't), obstinately determined to stay and not be tractored out, living off the land by catching rabbits, yet essentially lonely and glad of the company of Tom and Casy. He knows everything that is going on in the area, loves to talk of the past, and has some sense – the sense to know that he will destroy himself if he leaves what he cherishes.

Even those characters who enter our experience but once are stamped with quality: consider *Mae* in the snack-bar, flirting with the truck-drivers, bridling and aggressive, playing the role she feels is demanded of her, yet gruffly kind to the migrant and his children. Consider those truck-drivers; *Al* behind the bar; the wealthy but lonely couple who make boorishness their guard against feeling, and Hollywood gossip their stake in the future. Consider the abject self-pity of the one-eyed man at the spare-parts lot and Tom's attempt to give him back some dignity and reason for living; the fat man at the petrol station;

the manager of the government camp; the *Wainwrights* and their life in the box-car, with their concern for Aggie. There are others, passers-by, so to speak, in the text, but all felt and seen most clearly

This brings me to the triumph of Steinbeck's characterization. his ability to depict the old and the young with the careless ease of observed knowledge. *Grampa* and *Granma* exist in their tortured obstinacy, he in lechery and bloodymindedness, she in the religious ritual which makes her no less wicked. He eats, drinks, fights, struggles to button his flies, swears, the spirit of life strong in him: she fights, hallelujahs, amens, and once, after a meeting, 'she fired both barrels of a shotgun at her husband, ripping one of his buttocks nearly off'. It may seem strange to say, after this, that both are lovable, but they are: they, too, are victims of circumstance, both dying because they have been torn from their roots. They are balanced by *Ruth* and *Winfield*: jealous, confiding, fighting, telling tales; their exploration of the toilets at Weedpatch is a joy to read; while Ruthie's boasting about Tom puts the whole family in danger. They are real children seen in interaction. They are too young to be mindful of their roots, but the journey is as epic for them as it is for the others. When we finish the novel we are bound to think of Ruthie and Winfield; for their survival, and the marks of the journey upon them, are as important as anything in the book. The old die, but the young live on to endure and, perhaps, to fight.

Summaries of chapters, textual notes and revision questions

Note: Every effort has been made to keep these notes to a minimum. As the student reads on, he will become more familiar with the slang and colloquialisms of Steinbeck and, consequently, the later chapters are not so fully annotated as the earlier. Where a reference has not been fully defined, an approximation or short paraphrase has been given.

Chapter 1

The scene is set in Oklahoma, during a period of summer drought which affects the crops. There is the threat, but threat only, of rain; and this is followed by a windstorm that settles dust upon everything – a thick coating of it lies across the land. The women watch their menfolk 'figuring' what is to be done.

bayonet Finely economical way of describing the 'blade' of corn.
gullies i.e. water-worn ravines.
Gophers American burrowing rodents, ground squirrels.
ant lions Any of several insects whose larve lies hidden in a pit which it had dug. It preys on ants, insects etc.
milled Produced regular markings.
the Gulf Presumably a reference to the Gulf of Mexico.
the wind cried and whimpered over the fallen corn Superb personification, indicating the kinship between man and nature.
emulsion This is a milky liquid, but here it refers to the effect produced by the mixture of dust and air.
like pollen Ironic usage, since pollen is a means of fertilizing, but here there is no fertility in the life or the soil.
the sun was as red as ripe new blood Note again the irony as well as the vividness of the image – for there is no new blood here.
figuring i.e. working things out.

Chapter 2

The scene shifts to outside a small restaurant, where a roadside truck is standing. When the driver emerges he finds a hitchhiker waiting by his truck. Although it is against the rules, the driver gives him a lift. They get into conversation, with the driver trying to discover as much as he can about the hitchhiker, who reveals that his name is Tom Joad, and that his past four years have been spent in McAlester penitentiary, where he was sent for killing a man. Joad leaves the truck and sets off down the dirt road to look for his folks.

hasp A means of making fast or fastening.

stinko Drunk.

fender American word for bumper.

little clam shells A vivid comparison linking man and nature. Clams are shellfish, and the image is apt in the physical and emotional sense – Tom wears a protective 'shell' now that he is out of prison.

hams of his hands Palms.

callus Thickened part of skin or soft tissue.

visor Projecting front part of cap.

chambray A variety of gingham made by weaving white cotton threads across a coloured warp.

Diesel A type of oil engine named after the inventor, in which ignition of fuel is produced by the heat of air suddenly compressed.

cowl The top part at the front of an automobile body, to which the windscreen and dashboard are added.

nickels Five-cent pieces.

jackpot i.e. the biggest prize.

Three-eighty i.e. three dollars, 80 cents.

Tulsa City in Oklahoma.

Scrunch Squash.

My dogs was pooped out My feet were tired out.

to spread nets, to set traps with his questions The whole emphasis is on the driver's probing of Tom; he fancies himself as an amateur detective, and suspects that Tom has been in prison.

cropper A farmer who works another's land and receives a share of the crop.

dusted out . . . tractored out Driven out by the dust or by the tractors sent in by the landowners to clear the land.

cat Tractor.

truck skinner A driver.

screwin' around Being sexually promiscuous.

trigger Penis.

whanger Penis.

done it for ducks For the sake of saying something.

He wasn't puttin' on no dog He wasn't showing off.

sling the bull Boastful talk.

the broad Woman or girl (but used in a derogatory, cheap way, implying that she is no good).

goddamn cinch A complete certainty.

a snort A quick drink.

You're all wound up You're very tense.

no shot No drink (of whisky).

calloused Hardened, with calluses.

a goin' over You were interrogating me, trying to discover what you could.

I mind my own yard I look after my own concerns.

like a sheep in a vegetable patch An apt comparison. Sheep would have plenty to eat there, just as the driver has plenty to 'feed on' in probing Tom.

I done time I've been serving a sentence.

wettin' your pants i.e. getting excited.

I'm sprung in four for keeping my nose clean I've been released after four years for good behaviour.

in stir In prison.

spatted Slapped.

Chapter 3

This very brief chapter has a symbolic function in the novel: it describes the laborious journey of a land turtle by the roadside, the trials and tribulations it suffers, being missed by a car and deliberately hit by a truck. The turtle, like man, is overturned and, like man, rights itself.

the anlage The basis of a later development.
sow bugs like little armadillos Woodlice, like the burrowing mammals which have armour-like coverings of bony plates.
under brows like finger nails Linking of the animal and the human by this unobtrusive use of imagery.
A sedan An enclosed car which seats four or more people.
flipped the turtle like a tiddly-wink An image which finely expresses the casualness with which we do injury to others.
The humorous eyes The whole of this short chapter should be read as symbolic of the main action of the novel: the turtle's journey is the journey of the migrants, and the overturning and frustration it experiences is equivalent to the trials and tribulations of the Okies. The word 'humorous' even underlines, unconsciously since the turtle has only instinct, man's resilience in adversity.

Chapter 4

Tom Joad continues on his way, occasionally sipping whisky. All around him is the insidious dust, but he spies the turtle, picks it up and wraps it in his coat. He meets the ex-preacher, Jim Casy, who recognizes him and who is later to exert a profound influence on his life. They talk, partly of the past and Casy's obsession with the past temptations of the flesh; we see how human and vulnerable he is. Tom and he have an immediate feeling for each other, and both recall Tom's baptism at Casy's hands. Casy does not know of Tom's crime but Tom feels compelled to tell him about it. Eventually they reach the boundary fence of what both remember as the Joad property, but find the house itself deserted.

the blue air-shimmer The effects of distance and light accurately conveyed.

crotch i.e. a fork (here, one that supports the wire).

swale A hollow.

declivity Slope.

mussed Pushed roughly, disarranged.

sneakers American for tennis- or gym-shoes.

yankin' Pulling.

a Burning Busher Probably named after the plant, here meaning fiery, passionately religious.

just lousy with the spirit Full of religious ecstasy or feeling.

I rip out a meetin' Preach violently, sharply.

fact'ry liquor i.e. properly fermented and distilled, as distinct from home-made.

a buck A dollar.

plug . . . quid A piece of tobacco cut off for chewing . . . a lump of (tobacco) held in the mouth.

bulldozer The comparison here is with what is man-made – the turtle has to press on, overcoming obstacles, like a powerful caterpillar tractor.

talkin' in tongues i.e. talking volubly, when seized by religious ecstasy (a reference to Acts 2, 4).

pushin' 'em over Getting them in the mood (for making love).

Jehovites Strict and fervent religious sect.

mule-ass proof . . . fingerin' his pants buttons (Just when) you should be safe against sin . . . (you still) get the urge for sexual experience.

three-foot shag of bobwire A disordered, tangled mess.

coyote North American prairie dog.

shebang A particular matter of concern, affair, business.

eatin' on me Feeding on my mind, worrying me.

glory roof-tree . . . hunks of Jesus Filled with excess of religious feeling and inspiration.

plumb to squash Ironically, the description anticipates Casy's own death.

parole Freedom on the understanding that certain rules are kept.

purty Pretty.

drummer Travelling salesman.

stir-bug Prison companion (with a derogatory implication).

mosey along Go away, move along.

in a bug's age For a long time.

brang Brought.

too long a pecker Nose (but here perhaps with a more obscene implication, i.e. penis).

bolls The rounded seed-vessel of flax or cotton.

a dinger of a crop (It would have been) a very fine crop.

drug it Dragged it.

a litter of crap-houses The humour, though dirty, has a certain earthy imagination about it.

Jumpy as a stud horse i.e. anxious, restive for the mating with a mare.

freshet scars Made by the rushing of fresh water.

pray it set i.e. cure it, have it 'set' by praying.

shoat A young pig.

scairt Scared.

'Maybe Tom'll kill the fatted calf like for the prodigal in Scripture' See Luke, 15, 11–32.

bloat Swelling of the abdomen.

Chapter 5

This chapter provides background and foreground material to the plot, which deals with the migration of an individual family – the Joads. The attitudes of the owners – varying from cruelty to kindness – are stressed; with the banking and financial needs of the far distant background also bulking large in these local decisions. The men are told that they will have to get off the land, which is to be sold; and the tractors, sometimes encouraged to drive through farmsteads, arrive to plough up the land. Sometimes the drivers of these tractors are local men, forced, by their own need to survive, to undertake this work. So mechanization ultimately destroys what man created.

augers Instruments for boring into the soil, with stems that can be lengthened.

mathematics i.e. the calculations, the finances involving profit and loss.

scrabbed Scratched and dug (the soil), to try to get something out of it.

side-meat i.e. from the side of the pig. Bacon, salt pork.

hit the ceiling i.e. the top price will be obtained for it.

in the fall In the autumn.

crib Small bed for a child, with barred sides.

whale you i.e. wallop you, hit you.

having the incredible strength of insects The parallels with the natural and the man-made run throughout the novel, and here we are reminded of the ants and the ant lions.

gulches Ravines.

not ploughing but surgery A vividly effective image to indicate that an operation is being performed on the land, but that its growth is not being restored.

penes Plural of the penis, the male sex organ.

orgasms . . . raping methodically Continuation of the sexual image but with the assertion that the actions and the climaxes are mechanical, not imbued with physical passion.

Spam Tinned foodstuff, originating from the name of one of its ingredients, spiced ham.

a piece of pie branded like an engine part Steinbeck is intent on making the driver like his machine, and the image indicates automatic and mass preparation of food (like engine parts) as distinct from the individuality of home cooking.

sheathing Covering.

stringers Horizontal timbers connecting upright posts in a frame.

phalli The phallus is the image of the penis, symbolic of the generative power of nature; hence here it is a continuation of the sexual image and is being used ironically.

Chapter 6

Casy and Tom Joad inspect the deserted Joad farmhouse. The only sign of life is an old, grey cat. Tom and Casy reminisce, recalling family incidents and anecdotes. Tom releases the turtle he had picked up as a present, and Muley Graves appears on the scene. He gives Tom the news of his family's preparations to depart; he also provides their supper – three rabbits he has caught. Muley is lonely; he, too, talks of the past and tells them his own reasons for not leaving. All three dig up memories and all three feel the overwhelming need for human contact. Eventually Casy and Tom decide to go after Tom's family, but Muley obstinately refuses to accompany them. He has made himself a cave, in which he sleeps while the other two remain outside.

'Hell musta popped here' 'Something terrible must have happened'.

skittering Notice the onomatopoeic effect of the work which conveys the *noise* of sudden movement.

was in a family way i.e. pregnant.

touched Mentally unstable, a little mad.

throwing rocks i.e. stones thrown by children to break the windows.

Philadelphia *Ledger* Newspaper published in that city.

slat Thin, narrow piece of wood.

twelve-by-twelve i.e. measured in inches.

moulting Shedding.

a big jolt of the sperit A large amount of religious feeling.

lumber Disused articles of furniture, wood, etc.

winda Window.

squarin' off at him i.e. adopting an aggressive, attacking posture.

skunk A black, white-striped, bushy-tailed American carnivorous animal which emits a powerful smell from liquid secreted by anal glands.

squirt Insignificant, assertive or conceited man.

a gunny sack A sack of jute fibre.

stick her out i.e. stick it out, refuse to move.

la-de-da i.e. in an affected way.

choppin' cotton Weed or thin out young cotton.

jack-rabbits Large hares of Western North America, with long
  ears and strong hind legs.

smart-aleck Too clever, knowing too much (for your own good).

skin my life Run my life.

be quiet underground i.e. dead.

enough crop to plug up an ant's ass A very crude, but
  understandable, way of saying that the yield from the land has
  been very poor.

tin pedler i.e. selling pots and pans.

you could lay for Nobody you could put the blame on.

burned up Tired out.

fambly Family.

'coons Raccoons, greyish-grown carnivorous American nocturnal
  animals.

got a-holt Has grasped.

a snarl of bale wire Knotted, tangled.

hominy Coarsely ground maize boiled with water or milk.

'That's a daisy, that's a daisy' I suppose the best way to render
  this is 'What a beauty you are!'

huffy Offended, upset (with me).

a-bullin' Courting.

a straw boss i.e. in charge of the haymaking.

slug hell out of 'em i.e. set about them with your fists.

colder'n a wedge Knocked him out.

bresh (Muley's pronunciation of) brushwood.

Questions on chapters 1–6

1 What aspects of Steinbeck's style interest you most so far?
Quote in support of your views.

2 What kind of a man is (a) Tom Joad, and (b) Casy? Write a
short character sketch of each.

3 Write an account of the kind of humour to be found in these chapters.

4 How does Steinbeck maintain narrative tension?

5 Which aspect of the novel do you prefer so far: the 'perspective' chapters or those which deal with individuals? Give reasons and quote in support of your answer.

6 Indicate the importance of dialogue and dialect in the narrative so far.

Chapter 7

The emphasis in this chapter is on the sale of used cars to the migrants (the writing largely taking the form of dialogue), the bargaining, swindling, twisting dishonesty prevalent when need is great and quick profit is accordingly easy. Lists of cars punctuate the dialogue, which is imbued not only with the sharpness of the salesman but also with the pathos of the man who has to buy but has no idea of the value of what he is buying. This chapter by itself is an indictment of a way of life: increasing mechanization – and we have seen this earlier – puts man against man.

overhead No extra charges.
one and a quarter One dollar twenty-five cents.
Get 'em rolling Get them interested.
jalopy A dilapidated motor-car.
Sock it to 'em Give it to them squarely.
Cad . . . Buick . . . Ford . . . Nash Steinbeck uses lists of cars, some of which have survived to this day and are still being manufactured in contemporary styles, as a contrast to individual people who have become the slaves of the machines. (No attempt is made here to identify each make of car.)
a Hymie A shout, a call.
baloney Nonsense.

the upholstery is shot The seat covers are ruined.
cut Profit.
corral Capture, get hold of.
that lemon Something useless.
in the Monthly i.e. in a magazine advertising used cars.
a little snort a good stuff A short drink of good liquor.
bums i.e. vagrants, people who can't pay.
can that guy Sack that man.
to trade i.e. to exchange.
mules for nothing but glue Refers to the use of their hooves.
pikers People who are over cautious.
a sucker One who is easily made a fool of.
I got that team i.e. of mules.
kick through Pay up.
a dumb bunny Someone who is stupid.
jack in his jeans Money in his pockets.
sneaky Dishonest.
got a Elk's tooth Probably someone belonging to one of the
   benevolent orders or lodges. It may mean here someone rich or
   worth selling to.

Chapter 8

Tom and Casy set out in the wake of Tom's family, who are
thought to be staying with Uncle John prior to making their
way. They reach Uncle John's place and the first person they
see is Tom's father; then Tom is movingly reunited with his
mother and, later, with the rest of the family. Grampa,
Granma, his brothers Noah and Al, his sisters Ruthie and
'Rosasharn' (Rose of Sharon, now married to Connie Rivers)
and younger brother Winfield and, of course, Uncle John. To
Granma's delight, Casy says grace for them.

nuts Mad.
worms Parasites in the intestines.
feelin' purty fly Sexually excited.

cuss Curse.

iridescent Having the colours of the rainbow.

meerschaum Hydrous silicate of magnesium, found in soft white masses.

busted out Escaped.

Mother Hubbard A large shapeless dress.

arbiter i.e. one who judges, decides between.

a hammered sheep i.e. branded (to identify it).

a sledge A blacksmith's large, heavy hammer.

airship A dirigible, a flying machine lighter than air.

rot you out with crazy mad i.e. (nothing was done to you) that would make you embittered.

Her face looked for the answer that is always concealed in language A superbly economical way of indicating that the expression on a face conveys more than words.

varmint Vermin.

lobo A large grey timber wolf.

bulbous Like a bulb in shape.

member i.e. part of the body.

lay your sights i.e. set the sights (of your gun).

a heller Someone noisy, wild, reckless.

goin' to hell on a poker i.e. burning, the implication is 'quickly'.

fust First.

like Jesus went into the wilderness See Luke, 4, 1–2.

tinker an engine Understand the workings of the engine and correct faults.

billygoatin' . . . Tomcattin' . . . nuts Driven by sexual urges.

heifers Young girls.

squirtin' aroun' Playing about impudently, conceitedly.

Stetson Broad-brimmed slouch hat.

Chapter 9

This again digresses from the main plot concerning the Joad family, focusing on the tenants' having to sell up their equipment – for which they are paid rock-bottom prices – in order to raise enough money to move on.

guayule Aster-like American plant, the sap of which provides a rubber substitute.

hames Curved pieces of wood or metal forming part of the collar of a horse.

tugs Loops from the saddle supporting shaft or trace.

a drum-major The commander of drummers in a regiment, but now more commonly used at parades, marches, celebrations led by a man or a girl (drum-majorette) in uniform.

Pilgrim's Progress The famous Christian allegory by John Bunyan (1628–88).

St Louis Fair Celebrated fair, held regularly in that city.

Chapter 10

The truck is loaded and goes on ahead. Tom lingers in the now empty place, talking to his mother; they consider the journey to California, and the prospects they face on their arrival. Casy asks if he can go along with the family. When the truck returns we learn of the guilt feelings of Uncle John over the death of his young, pregnant wife many years ago. All the men are dispirited, since they have succeeded in raising only eighteen dollars on their equipment. The family council is held that evening. Casy is admitted afterwards, and is allowed to travel on with them. The men slaughter the pigs in order to take salted pork on the journey; Casy helps Ma salt down the meat. Granpa then refuses to go with them but is dosed with Winfield's soothing medicine; and the family set off, leaving Muley 'standing forlornly in the door-yard', looking after them.

lean-to Built against the side of the house, that is, leaning against it.

snitch a little ratty one Steal one that was inferior to the others.

'Don't roust your faith bird-high an' you won't do no crawlin' with the worms.' Don't build up your hopes too much, and you won't find that you are too badly disappointed.

par'ble Parable.

bein' in the pen Being in prison.

get dry behin' the ears (When you) grow up.

a single-action Colt Automatic revolver named after the inventor.

he cuckoo'd 'em i.e. he left somebody else to bring them up, just as a cuckoo leaves its eggs in other birds' nests.

sun-shook Sun-stroke.

much A kind of porridge.

Salvation Army Organization on military model intent on the revival of religion among the masses, founded by General Booth (1829–1912).

'we'd a drawed solitary' 'We'd have been put in solitary confinement.'

smack ya in the puss Hit you in the face.

kid-wild and calfish The comparisons are relatively obvious, but they underline yet again Steinbeck's linking of man and nature.

hoyden Boisterous girl.

jake Alcoholic extract of Jamaican ginger.

a musking goat i.e. randy, eager to mate.

Merchandizing Trading, buying and selling.

blowin' off Talking big.

get 'im bore Have him born.

stereopticon A magic lantern having a powerful projecting light, especially one using double pictures, each with a separate lens, for producing dissolving views.

squidged Squelched.

skinned Swindled.

ornery Obstinate, mean.

a-fartin' aroun' like a dog-wolf i.e. chasing all the girls.

shut of Rid of.

carborundum stone A compound of carbon and silicon used for sharpening or polishing by abrasion.

singletrees Wooden bars at the centre from a hitch on a plough, hooked at either end to the traces of horses' harness.

rat-tail files i.e. those having tapering ends, like rats' tails.

'God in the buckboard' A colloquial expression, a buckboard
  being the body of a cart.
tar'd Tired.
dust mice Probably small clusters of fluff resembling mice in
  shape.
they boosted him i.e. gave him a boost by half carrying him.

Chapter 11

An interim chapter, describing the empty houses and land,
and the gradual effects of dust and decay in the deserted
houses.

nitrates . . . phosphates . . . carbon Again, a listing, like that of
  the cars earlier. Here the list consists of chemical definitions of the
  composition of the land; the irony is that the land itself and man
  himself are more than all these.
shingle Rectangular strip of wood used as roof-tile.

Chapter 12

This chapter starts with an account of the 'main migrant road'
– Highway 66. Again it is in the form of dialogue, this time
between members of migrant families on the long trek to
California with their patched-up vehicles, their short supplies,
their worries about what they will find when they get there.
This is a description of the many before we return to the one
whose route we are to take – the truck driven by Al Joad.

the Divide Dividing ridge or section of high ground between two
  basins or areas of drainage.
ol' jub Derogatory term for describing the truck.
real estate Houses, property.
who's gettin' screwed? Who is being swindled?

Questions on chapters 7–12

1 What do you find disturbing about Chapter 7 (the used-car-lot)? Give reasons for your answer, and write a short appreciation of Steinbeck's main technique in this chapter.

2 Describe, in some detail, the various members of the Joad family. What elements of sadness *or* humour do you find in them?

3 How does Steinbeck make his own sympathies known to you in these chapters? Quote in support of your views.

4 Write an essay on Steinbeck's use of imagery in these chapters, with particular reference to natural and man-made associations.

Chapter 13

The Joads find that they have forgotten their water, and have to pull into a petrol station to get some. They also fill up with petrol, and realize that the petrol attendant is in the same uncertain state as they are themselves. They resume their journey, but not before their dog is run over. Later they stop by the side of the road and meet the Wilsons, who are to join them in this phase of the journey. Grampa is obviously very ill, suffers a stroke and dies in the Wilson tent, nursed at the end by Sairy Wilson. They make a grave, and Casy says a few words over the body. Joads and Wilsons join for the next part of the journey, Ma and Sairy having formed a strong sympathetic bond.

baby buggies Perambulators.
sound off at ya Shout at you.
Gila monsters Large venomous lizards of New Mexico and Arizona.
Give me a start Suddenly upset me.
oil derricks Frameworks over oil wells or borings.

a bigger folt'n other folks More severely punished than the others.

sombrero Broad-brimmed straw or felt hat, more common in Latin America.

a stroke Paralysis or apoplexy, a sudden disabling attack.

no beholden in a time of dying (There's no) owing anything when death is with us.

to sift the law i.e. examine it, inspect it carefully.

He died the minute you took 'im off the place A poignant reminder of the effect on the old people of the enforced migration. Granma is to die later.

Chapter 14

Very brief chapter dealing with the era of change and the need for man to find himself and organize himself, with the main theme embodied in the following quotation: 'For the quality of owning freezes you forever into "I", and cuts you off forever from the "we" '.

zygote Product of the fusion of two gametes (sexual bodies which unite with others for reproduction). Here the implication is that the one joins with another until they become the many, that is 'I' becomes 'we'.

Chapter 15

A hamburger-stand on Highway 66. First Mae behind the counter, then a discontented rich couple, then the truck-drivers, then the migrant with two small sons, who has pride but little money. Mae and the truck-drivers and Al, the chef, prove to have hearts of gold.

'Ti-pi-ti-pi-tin' . . . 'Thanks for the Memory' Two popular songs of the late nineteen-thirties.

Bing Crosby The popular singer, or crooner (b. 1904).

Benny Goodman The swing and jazz clarinetist and band leader (b. 1909).

Seltzer Originally from the medicinal mineral water of Selters in Germany, but there are many artificial substitutes for this.

mica One of several minerals found in small, glittering scales in granite or in crystals.

Butts A pun on 'cigarette ends' and 'bottoms'.

a Pet i.e. don't let her do the cooking, keep her for petting (caressing).

burlap Coarse canvas.

spatula A broad-bladed instrument, here used for removing grease.

quoit Heavy, flattish, sharp-edge iron ring thrown to encircle an iron peg or stick.

it ain't got the sap It hasn't got the power.

accoutrements Equipment, trappings.

cases of rubber Corsets, foundation garments.

Beverly–Wiltshire Hotel . . . Trocadero Celebrated society hotel, club restaurant.

syphilis Venereal disease.

crab Grumble.

Java Coffee.

slugs Pieces of metal shaped like coins and used in place of them.

seen any new etchin's Sexual innuendo, meaning 'Have you had any good times lately?'

You can have her for peanuts now You can have her very cheaply.

rum-dumb Rhyming slang for 'silent'.

roached Cut short all over.

greasy bills i.e. much thumbed dollar notes.

Chapter 16

The Joads and Wilsons move across Texas. Rose of Sharon dreams of how she and Connie will live in a house and own a store; the Wilson car breaks down and Tom offers to stay behind with Casy and bring it on later. But Ma takes an opposite view, and wins the day by refusing to move unless they all go together. Al goes in to town to get the spare part needed, and Tom and Casy talk together and leave the family at a camp. Granma has now become unwell. Al and Tom talk, too, and Al reveals to Tom how worried Ma is about him. Al and Tom go to a wrecking-yard, where they meet a one-eyed man; he is embittered by his maiming, but they get the parts they want at very little cost. They go back, fix up the truck and then go to where the family are camping. The proprietor wants to charge them for staying; and they also meet a ragged man who has come back from California, where he has lost his wife and their two children. He describes the appalling nature of cheap labour there.

convulsions Violent and irregular motions of limbs and body due to an involuntary contraction of the muscles.

foetus The embryo in the womb.

pitchers Pictures, that is, the cinema.

the structure i.e. the face, and the developing expression.

pan i.e. cooked in a pan.

whup me Knock me about.

'I'll light into you.' 'I'll set about you, I'll fight you.'

'I'll knock you belly-up with a bucket.' Roughly speaking, this means 'I'll hit you so hard you'll be flat on your back.'

sassy Saucy.

a-pawin' for a shovel herself i.e. asking to be buried because she is so ill. Of course Granma is not doing this, and there is a kind of grim humour in the statement.

bar-arn Iron bar.

filled her flush i.e. with excitement, anger, had a sudden rush of emotion.

'I was smokin' Sexually excited.

cantaloupe A kind of melon.

babbitt Soft alloy of tin, antimony and copper.

they turned the numbers back i.e. they faked the mileage that was registered, making it appear less than it was.

shims Wedges used to make parts fit.

hell of a bang . . . tryin' to roll out He was thrilled by it . . . what are you trying to say?

tarp Abbreviation for 'tarpaulin'.

sell ya a little tank a air Heavily ironic condemnation of the profit motive.

crap a litter a lizards Very vulgar way of saying (Pa) would be very angry.

go down the line i.e. clear off.

stir-nuts Mad from being in prison.

for wore For wear.

whang him Hit him hard.

'Whyn't you roll on?' 'Why don't you clear out, move?'

got a hard row A hard life.

'Tell 'em ya dong's growed sence you los' your eye.' Tom can be coarse at times, particularly when he is angry. The reference is to the male sexual organ.

'if you put up a squawk' Object strongly.

'Figgers how bad ya need it' Works out how essential it is to you.

I'm gonna take a fall outa you . . . jus' scrabblin' ass over tit' I'm going to put you in your place . . . you're just too concerned (with not having the blame put on you').

they gonna sock ya i.e. charge you.

'That's his screwin'' That's his worry.

'I like to starved' I was very hungry.

pig lucky Very fortunate.

off her chump Touched in the head, mad.

with my mitts With my fists.

jump Jesus Take a risk, tempt providence.

all over at oncet Completely now, all at once.

fret you Worry you.

jackassin' Playing about.

a labour faker Presumably a term applied to those who were talking of labour conditions at the time and influencing their fellows.

scary an' nimsy-mimsy Nervous and over-anxious.

half bucks rollin' down the road. No more money coming in tonight (in the form of more poor families in trucks).

bolshevisky Communist, the word coming from the Russian meaning 'majority party'.

Chapter 17

This describes the camps formed on the road, where a spirit of comradeship is to be found; where families merge into small communities having their own codes of behaviour and loyalty. Always there are the reminiscences, and the coming together in the evenings for the sing-songs led by the guitar player.

torn down like a circus This indicates the transitory nature of the life of the migrants, with a constant moving on.

a potter's field A burial ground for poverty-stricken, friendless or unknown people.

bound with acres . . . narrow concrete miles A deliberate contrast between what man has as his inheritance and what man has made.

fool's gold Copper pyrites, which is like gold in colour.

bigges' old son-a-bitchin' This simply means 'the largest'.

Dutch-oven biscuits Made in an iron kettle, used for baking. It has a convex lid on which live coals can be placed.

gullied up on ya Dried up, unable to form gullies (of water).

'cordeen Accordion.

withers The ridge between a horse's shoulder-blades.

a picker One who can play a tune note by note.

don't get hung up i.e. stranded.

She'll cut the living Jesus outa you (Crossing the desert) will exhaust you and the truck.

Chapter 18

The Joads pass through New Mexico and climb into the high country of Arizona. Then they have to cross the desert. They stop to bathe, and meet two men on their way back who confirm the ragged man's account of life in California. They also tell them how they – the 'Okies' – will be treated there with contempt; at this juncture Noah decides that he will not go on with the rest of the family. Meanwhile Granma is very ill, and one of the women in the camp insists on organizing a prayer meeting on her behalf, though Ma makes them hold it in one of their own tents and not near Granma. Later a policeman appears in Ma's tent, and threatens to run them all out of the camp if they don't move on in the morning. Ma confides this and her worries on his account to Tom. They decide to go on immediately, but Sairy Wilson is too ill to move, and Casy takes a compassionate farewell of her. They leave Wilson, but not before giving him some money, pork and potatoes. They drive across the desert at night: Connie and Rose of Sharon make love, the truck is stopped but allowed on, and Ma tells the others that Granma has died.

a tule A large bulrush.
shucked off their pants Removed them.
the scales ain't honest i.e. they don't give the true weight.
puckering Contracting into wrinkles.
kil't Killed.
can't he cut her? i.e. get something to do.
set on our tail Sit down and relax (at home).
lonely and away i.e. (having a baby) is your experience and yours only.
fly all apart i.e. give way, lose my temper.
feral howling Wild, untamed, brutal howling.
hyena Carnivorous animal allied to the dog tribe, with a howl like laughter.
epaulets Ornamental shoulder-pieces of uniform.
Sam Browne An army officer's belt and straps, named after (The British) General Sir S. J. Browne.
skillet Small metal pot with long handle used in cooking.

a tin button A badge.

musk-rat Large North American aquatic rodent, notable for its
  fur.

Jenny Lind Known as 'the Swedish Nightingale'; famous, world-
  travelled singer.

cut the coupon This would be filled in and sent and in return
  details would be received of the study courses.

eucalyptus Genus of plants which includes the gum tree.

heliograph A signalling apparatus reflecting flashes of sunlight.

comforter A woollen scarf.

the hump . . . the steep cliff Notice how Granma in death is
  compared to nature, thus establishing the link between human
  and physical nature yet again.

get aholt of 'im (I) can't get close to him.

resinous sage Aromatic herb.

Chapter 19

This chapter opens with an historical account of California, its
agricultural development and how it has attracted migrants in
the past as well as the present; restrictions against them,
however, are such that the big owners prevent them getting on
to the land in order to work it. Pressures within California
build up against the migrants, who are thought of as foreign-
ers, cop-killers, people with whom one takes no chances.
The squatters' camps are called Hoovervilles, and in them
disease through malnutrition is common. But that same community spirit seen earlier is often present – the poor seek to
alleviate the suffering of their brothers.

Sutter's land, Guerrero's land A reference to John Sutter, who
  owned a mill north-east of Sacramento in California; gold was
  first discovered near there in 1848. The second reference is to a
  state in south-west Mexico.

chittering Notice the onomatopoeic quality of the word.

to replenish i.e. to replace the chemicals which had been taken out of the soil.

Hooverville Presumably an ironic way of indicating that it was subject to investigation. J. Edgar Hoover was Director of the Federal Bureau of Investigation.

raft A large number.

Jimson weeds Poisonous plants of the nightshade family.

the Lombards did in Italy, as the Germans did on Gaul and the Turks did on Byzantium The Lombards invaded Italy in AD 568, and conquered the north in three years, later becoming themselves Italianized; the Teutonic tribes subdued Gaul (France), establishing powerful kingdoms in Europe which lasted until the sixth and seventh centuries. Byzantium, the ancient name for Constantinople, was founded by the Greeks in 667 BC. It fell to the Turks in 1453.

congressmen Members of the national legislative body of the United States of America.

stew bums Vagrants, tramps, from the lowest, most sordid levels of society.

blaster Presumably an enema, to enable him to pass the worms.

black-tongue Identified with pellagra in man, associated with diet deficiency.

county stone orchard i.e. graveyard.

Questions on chapters 13–19

1 Write a detailed account of the scene in the snack-bar and say what it tells you of human nature.

2 Indicate the part played in this section by Sairy Wilson.

3 What aspects of the narrative do you find either pathetic or tragic in this part of the novel?

4 In what ways is Ma the most important person in the Joad family? You should quote in support of your answer.

5 What aspects of Steinbeck's art do you find most absorbing? Refer closely to the text in your answer.

Chapter 20

This chapter opens with the family outside the coroner's office in Bakersfield. A county burial is arranged for Granma, and then the family go to a ramshackle camp. Again they are enlightened, this time by a young camp resident, about the poor pay they can expect if they are successful in getting a job. He also reveals that the police visit the camp frequently and deal with 'trouble-makers', i.e. those who are trying to stand together and obtain a fair deal for themselves. Casy and Tom determine to go out and look for work the next day, but Connie is beginning to wish that he had not come with them. Another resident tells of government camps which are well run and have modern facilities. A contractor arrives, offering the men poorly paid work, but he will not disclose what that pay is; a row breaks out. The accompanying police back the contractor, and one of them after shooting off a woman's knuckles, is stunned by Casy. Tom has previously tripped the deputy, but Casy gets him away and then gives himself up to the police. Meanwhile Connie runs away, Uncle John gets drunk, Tom brings him back to the family and they set off again – only to be stopped by men wearing American Legion caps. The Joads are turned back, but make a detour in order to get on to their original route.

sidewalks Pavements.
nutser'n me Madder than I am.
tuckered out Exhausted.
bull-simple A reference to the stupidity of the bull, how it keeps on doing the same things – consider its behaviour in the bull-ring, for example, when it constantly returns to the matador's goading.

compound A mixture (but here it is not clear what the mixture consists of).

to a nub To a small knob or lump.

That's stinkin' That is disgraceful, disgusting.

the blacklist i.e. a list of people who are known troublemakers or who are supporters of a particular cause that is regarded with disfavour.

a nice job a pickin' A good repair job.

kinkin' Twisting.

sack a Durham Pouch of tobacco.

jigger Handle.

cor'ner The coroner.

tore-down car i.e. one with the engine stripped down.

han'holt . . . han'turn Both references to 'There's no work to be had.'

a piece For a while.

it's keyed to the price i.e. related to the cost.

talkin' red Speaking like a Communist.

float 'em quick Soon get rid of them.

tourniquet A way of stopping the flow of blood through an artery by compression, tying tightly.

git aholt Pull yourself together.

candyin' yaself Spoiling yourself.

champagny water Champagne, not very strong alcohol.

to make a pinch An arrest.

American Legion Generally associated with veterans of World War I.

Chapter 21

A brief chapter describing the general swarming of the migrant families across the West, with the reactions against the 'Okies' of the local people being stressed. Human suffering is the result of the exploitation methods employed by the owners of canneries and granaries.

agrarian i.e. those who cultivated the land.

paradoxes Statements contrary to received opinion, here
meaning the apparent contradictions in the industrial way of life.

bloated up Swelled up.

a cannery A factory where fruit is canned by mechanical
processes.

rachitic Rickets, a disease in children, involving softening of the
bones – particularly of the spine – and bow legs.

pustules of pellagra Wart-like excrescences in a deficiency
disease which is characterized by cracking of the skin.

Chapter 22

Tom drives through the night to the Weedpatch government
camp. He makes friends with two men who find him a job,
although again the rate is very poor. There is considerable
anti-red agitation in the area against the existence of the
camp; the latter is administered by a central committee.
Meanwhile, the children try the (to them) luxury toilets and
Ma is visited by the kindly and enlightened camp manager.
The camp is well organized and run on the basis of communal
responsibility. Meanwhile, Rose of Sharon continues to brood
on the departure of Connie, and the committee of ladies comes
to see Ma. Afterwards Ma has a row with an interfering and
narrow-minded woman who falls into a fit. Pa and Uncle John
do not succeed in finding work.

boulevard Broad street with rows of trees.

the tiny marks Points or prongs (of the rake).

a little charge account i.e. credit facilities.

muck-stick man i.e. someone capable of doing the dirty work.

winery Where wine is made.

a picket A stake.

a-kyoodlin' aroun' Going out and having a good time.

a-snootin' Being inquisitive.

Pone A cake of stiff cornmeal batter.

he fit in He fought in the . . .

Oxfords Low shoes lacing over the instep.

clutch-an'-hug dancin' i.e. dancing very close together.

a-reelin' Swinging, swaying, lurching about.

deep-down lamb-blood Full of religious fervour and belief.

is puttin' nothin' over on God Fooling or misleading God.

tech Touch.

ruint 'count of Ruined because they (were play-acting).

redd Tidied up.

too big for his overhalls Too conceited, too concerned with his own doings.

shucks Valueless beings.

dray-horse Large and powerful horse. A dray is a brewer's cart.

Skitters Diarrhoea.

the Aid i.e. government assistance.

tree Find.

My dogs is wore Another of the many expressions indicating the tiredness (in the feet) of those who tramp about looking for work.

I didn' give 'em brain room . . . now they're aflockin' back I didn't think of them before, but now they're haunting my memory.

Wedgin' south . . . they're awful dinky Flying south (in formation) . . . they're very pretty.

Chapter 23

Again, a general account of the migrant people and their craving for amusement in the camps along the road – the story-telling, the anecdotes, the harmonica and guitar-playing which makes for relaxation and the temporary banishment of worries. And always a preacher with his small flock of devotees who are 'saved'.

Geronimo (1829–1909). American chief of the Apache tribe.

you spoiled somepin better'n you Something more perfect than you are, in this instance the cock pheasant.

radical meetin' Attended by people pressing for reforms.

uppity Haughty, arrogant.

German soliders kickin' up their feet Goose-stepping, raising their feet stiffly and high.

harmonica Mouth-organ.

frets Bars or ridges on fingerboards of some stringed instruments fixing positions of fingers to produce the required notes.

rosin Resin, adhesive substance insoluble in water, secreted by most plants and exuding naturally, or upon incision, from the fir or pine tree.

skirl Strictly speaking, this is the sound characteristic of the bagpipes.

haycock Conical heap of hay.

Chapter 24

Word has got around that the agitators are going to try to break up the Saturday night dance at the camp by infiltrating trouble-makers into the camp. Some get in, but a group of the campers, including Tom, see them off the site.

draws subsidies i.e. are allocated money by the state in order to help them function.

'They're doin' stuff got to be done' They're doing essential work.

dol ce do Sweet and soft (words in a call made by the square-dance caller).

Chapter 25

This opens with a lyrical account of spring in California as things begin to grow, but it continues with a description of over-ripening, rot and waste. What is grown is guarded and must not be touched, while people die of malnutrition. The chapter ends with the symbolic title of the novel coming to fruition: 'In the souls of the people the grapes of wrath are filling and growing heavy, growing heavy for the vintage.'

yellow-jackets Any of several wasps or hornets having bright yellow markings.

formic acid . . . sulphur . . . tannic acid A colourless irritant contained in fluid emitted by ants, pale yellow non-metallic element (burning with a stifling smell) and an astringent substance chiefly obtained from the bark of oak, etc.

putrescence Decaying matter, rotting, gone bad.

Questions on chapters 20–25

1 Compare and contrast the government camp with that of Hooverville.

2 What aspects of Steinbeck's style do you find poetic?

3 Write an appreciation of any two dramatic scenes in this section.

4 Indicate the part played by Rose of Sharon and Al in the story.

Chapter 26

Ma urges decision on the rest of the family – only Tom has managed to find any work and they are now living on fried dough. Ma's main concern is for Winfield and, of course, Rose of Sharon. The Joads rise before dawn and head on up north; unfortunately they get a puncture, but while they are changing the wheel a man approaches, and says there is work for peach pickers farther on. The family arrives at the Hooper ranch, only to be stopped by the police because there is trouble there. They go in and are signed on to pick peaches at five cents a box. Ma buys provisions at the camp store, where there is considerable overcharging.

Meanwhile, at night, Tom gets outside the camp fence and meets Casy, who tells him that he and his friends are picketing the camp, acting together in order to be allowed the freedom to make their own deals for pay. Casy tells Tom to influence the people inside, and urge them not to work for a pittance. But the picket breakers are out and Casy is killed by one of them with a pick handle; Tom, incensed, kills the murderer, and flees. He is injured, and though he gets back to the camp, the extent of his injuries is revealed in the morning. The family realize what has happened; and Tom is smuggled out in the truck as they 'migrate' once more. This time they go to the cotton-picking area, where Tom decides to hide in a culvert; and the family live in a box-car.

a-treadin' him on i.e. forcing him to respond, forcing him to show that he still has some spirit left.

Gettin' so tightful it's a-pullin' her eyes wide The implication is that she is so distended (with carrying the baby) that her eyes are getting wider apart.

snuck off Sneaked off.

a-stewin' aroun' Fuming, angry within myself.

all-nighter i.e. a restaurant which stays open throughout the night.

I was gonna lay for him I was going to wait an opportunity (to attack him).

a screwball Someone who is mad or unbalanced.

The pall i.e. the misery of their situation. A pall is a cloth spread over a coffin.

sateen Cotton fabric with glossy, satin-like surface.

to act flip Saucy, impertinent.

spark-plugging the thing Stirring things up, setting things going.

J. P. Morgan John Pierpoint Morgan, American financier who carried through a large number of industrial deals, including the establishment of the U.S. Steel Corporation. (1837–1913).

cut the rate here i.e. lower the pay.

Washington . . . Fit the Revolution George Washington, founder of the United States and its first President, led the revolt against the mother country. (1732–1799).

Lincoln Abraham Lincoln, sixteenth President of the United States, fought the Civil War successfully against the Southern states, proclaimed the emancipation of the negro slaves, was re-elected President but assassinated by John Wilkes Booth, the actor. (1809–1865).

a-hankerin' an' a-jibbitin' Wanting and fretting to go (away).

Winchester ·38 A type of repeating rifle named after the inventor.

slupped Spilled.

Roust! Stir, get up.

crick Creek.

Chapter 27

Now an interim chapter, again largely in dialogue, on cotton picking: its nature, the work involved and the payment; all as a prelude to the Joad family's working in the fields.

gin A machine for separating cotton from its seeds.

compress Apparatus for squeezing.

clods Earth (here used to make the bag of 'cotton' weigh more).

Chapter 28

The Joads live in one end of a box-car. For a while they live well, able to get meat and the milk needed for Rose of Sharon. Ruthie gives the game away to another child that Tom is in hiding. Ma goes out to Tom with some food; they say a moving good-bye and Ma returns to the box-car, where Al later appears, to tell them he is going to marry Aggie Wainwright. There is a small party in celebration; but Rose of Sharon is somewhat upset, and the next day insists on going cotton picking. The family, together with the other pickers, go into the field, but by now rain is threatening. They drive back to the box-car, having picked as much as they can; Rose of Sharon begins to feel ill.

droolin' Slobbering.

snotty Annoyed, short-tempered.

cleated cat-walk Wedges on the steep steps.

a cricking downpour Onomatopoeic word to describe the noise of the rain on the leaves.

effluvium Smell.

squirrelin' i.e. hiding, storing.

Howdy How do you do.

patina Gloss produced by age.

dunghill rooster i.e. has to display his masculinity.

jumped Surprised.

Chapter 29

This is a brief chapter which describes the onset of the rain and its effects – the ruining of cars, crops, the arrival of illness and disease. Flooding is followed by fear, anger, hunger.

mastoids An abscess on the temporal bone behind each ear.

Chapter 30

The effects of the rain and the subsequent flooding are felt in the box-car camp. The men have no work to do, for there is none for them. The Joads and the Wainwrights try to build a bank against the flood waters. Meanwhile, Rose of Sharon begins to have her baby. The flood breaks through and puts the truck out of action. When the men return to the car they find that Rose of Sharon has given birth to a stillborn child. After the ordeal, and with the water creeping up all around them, Ma decides that they must move to higher ground. They move on up the road and eventually come to a rain-soaked barn. Inside they find a starving man and a boy, and the novel closes with Rose of Sharon giving her breast to the man in order to save him. Thus we end with a question-mark; the Joads may not survive, but in a world which has used them ill they continue to act, through the driving force of Ma, with humanity and compassion for those worse off than themselves.

Rochester lamp Presumably originating from Rochester, a city in New York State.
paring Shaving, cutting away.
levee Embankment against river floods.
In a pig's eye The general meaning is 'I don't believe you.'
puked Was sick.
her lips came together and smiled mysteriously The implication is that she is dreaming that her motherhood has been fulfilled.

Questions on chapters 26–30

1 What do you find degrading about life at the Hooper ranch?

2 Write a dramatic account of Tom's meeting with Casy. How would you define Casy's views?

3 In what ways has Steinbeck prepared us for the ending? Do you find it effective, or not?

4 Write an appreciation of Steinbeck's use of contrast in this section.

5 Which of these chapters do you consider the most realistic? In your answer, give supporting reasons from the text.

General questions

1 Write a detailed character sketch of Ma, and indicate the influence she has on her family and on others in the novel.

2 Describe the part played in *The Grapes of Wrath* by the past, and indicate its influence on the lives of any *three* of the characters.

3 Trace the development of the character of Tom Joad. To what extent do you consider that he is the hero of *The Grapes of Wrath*?

4 In what ways do you find Casy either real or idealized in the novel? Quote in support of your answer.

5 Indicate the part played by the author himself in his novel. How far does Steinbeck's voice influence your response to the themes of *The Grapes of Wrath*?

6 What are the main themes of the novel? In your answer, refer closely to the text.

7 What part is played by nature in the structure of the novel?

8 Write an essay on Steinbeck's use of imagery in *The Grapes of Wrath*.

9 Trace the journey of the Joad family from Uncle John's to the box-car. What, for you, are the most significant events of this journey?

10 Write an essay on the types of humour employed by Steinbeck in *The Grapes of Wrath*.

11 Describe how the migration affects the old and the young in the novel.

12 'A morbid book'. Is this a fair reflection of the content and action of *The Grapes of Wrath*?

13 What evidence is there in the novel that there is political (and other) agitation against the 'Okies'?

14 Write an essay on Steinbeck's use either of monologue or dialogue in *The Grapes of Wrath*.

15 What factors make *The Grapes of Wrath* a great novel, *or* write an essay on the limitations of *The Grapes of Wrath*.

16 In what ways does the title of the novel indicate Steinbeck's purpose?

17 What does *The Grapes of Wrath* tell you about human nature? You may limit yourself or two or three facets in your answer.

18 Write an essay on any satirical or ironic aspects of Steinbeck's art in this novel.

19 What part does religion play in *The Grapes of Wrath*?

20 'Essentially a visual novel'. How far would you agree with this assessment of *The Grapes of Wrath*?

Pan study aids Titles published in the Brodie's Notes series

W. H. Auden Selected Poetry

Jane Austen Emma Mansfield Park Northanger Abbey Persuasion
Pride and Prejudice

Anthologies of Poetry Ten Twentieth Century Poets The Poet's
Tale

Samuel Beckett Waiting for Godot

Arnold Bennett The Old Wives' Tale

William Blake Songs of Innocence and Experience

Robert Bolt A Man for All Seasons

Harold Brighouse Hobson's Choice

Charlotte Brontë Jane Eyre

Emily Brontë Wuthering Heights

Robert Browning Selected Poetry

John Bunyan The Pilgrim's Progress

Geoffrey Chaucer (parallel texts) The Franklin's Tale The Knight's
Tale The Miller's Tale The Nun's Priest's Tale The Pardoner's Tale
Prologue to the Canterbury Tales The Wife of Bath's Tale

Richard Church Over the Bridge

John Clare Selected Poetry and Prose

Samuel Taylor Coleridge Selected Poetry and Prose

Wilkie Collins The Woman in White

William Congreve The Way of the World

Joseph Conrad The Nigger of the Narcissus & Youth The Secret
Agent

Charles Dickens Bleak House David Copperfield Dombey and Son
Great Expectations Hard Times Little Dorrit Oliver Twist
Our Mutual Friend A Tale of Two Cities

Gerald Durrell My Family and Other Animals

Georg Eliot Middlemarch The Mill on the Floss Silas Marner

T. S. Eliot Murder in the Cathedral

Henry Fielding Joseph Andrews

F. Scott Fitzgerald The Great Gatsby

E. M. Forster Howard's End A Passage to India
Where Angels Fear to Tread

William Golding Lord of the Flies The Spire

Oliver Goldsmith Two Plays of Goldsmith: She Stoops to Conquer;
The Good Natured Man

Graham Greene Brighton Rock The Power and the Glory

Thom Gunn and Ted Hughes Selected Poems

Thomas Hardy Chosen Poems of Thomas Hardy
Far from the Madding Crowd Jude the Obscure
The Mayor of Casterbridge Return of the Native
Tess of the d'Urbervilles The Trumpet-Major

L. P. Hartley The Go-Between The Shrimp and the Anemone

Joseph Heller Catch-22

Ernest Hemingway For Whom the Bell Tolls
The Old Man and the Sea

Barry Hines A Kestrel for a Knave

Gerard Manley Hopkins Poetry and Prose of Gerard Manley
Hopkins

Aldous Huxley Brave New World

Henry James Washington Square

Ben Johnson The Alchemist Volpone

James Joyce A Portrait of the Artist as a Young Man

John Keats Selected Poems and Letters of John Keats

Ken Kesey One Flew over the Cuckoo's Nest

Rudyard Kipling Kim

D. H. Lawrence The Rainbow Selected Tales Sons and Lovers

Harper Lee To Kill a Mockingbird

Laurie Lee As I Walked out One Midsummer Morning
Cider with Rosie

Thomas Mann Death in Venice & Tonio Kröger

Christopher Marlowe Doctor Faustus Edward the Second

W. Somerset Maugham Of Human Bondage

Arthur Miller The Crucible Death of a Salesman

John Milton A Choice of Milton's Verse Comus and Samson
Agonistes Paradise Lost I, II

Sean O'Casey Juno and the Paycock The Shadow of a Gunman and The Plough and the Stars

George Orwell Animal Farm 1984

John Osborne Luther

Alexander Pope Selected Poetry

Siegfried Sassoon Memoirs of a Fox-Hunting Man

Peter Shaffer The Royal Hunt of the Sun

William Shakespeare Antony and Cleopatra As You Like It Coriolanus Hamlet Henry IV (Part I) Henry IV (Part II) Henry V Julius Caesar King Lear King Richard III Love's Labour Lost Macbeth Measure for Measure The Merchant of Venice A Midsummer Night's Dream Much Ado about Nothing Othello Richard II Romeo and Juliet The Sonnets The Taming of the Shrew The Tempest Twelfth Night The Winter's Tale

G. B. Shaw Androcles and the Lion Arms and the Man Caesar and Cleopatra The Doctor's Dilemma Pygmalion Saint Joan

Richard Sheridan Plays of Sheridan: The Rivals; The Critic; The School for Scandal

John Steinbeck The Grapes of Wrath Of Mice and Men & The Pearl

Tom Stoppard Rosencrantz and Guildenstern are Dead

J. M. Synge The Playboy of the Western World

Jonathan Swift Gulliver's Travels

Alfred Tennyson Selected Poetry

William Thackeray Vanity Fair

Flora Thompson Lark Rise to Candleford

Dylan Thomas Under Milk Wood

Anthony Trollope Barchester Towers

Mark Twain Huckleberry Finn

Keith Waterhouse Billy Liar

Evelyn Waugh Decline and Fall

H. G. Wells The History of Mr Polly

John Webster The White Devil

Oscar Wilde The Importance of Being Earnest

Virginia Woolf To the Lighthouse

William Wordsworth The Prelude (Books 1, 2)
Wordsworth Selections

W. B. Yeats Selected Poetry

Australian titles

George Johnston My Brother Jack

Thomas Keneally The Chant of Jimmie Blacksmith

Ray Lawler Summer of the Seventeenth Doll

Henry Lawson The Bush Undertaker & Selected Short Stories

Ronald McKie The Mango Tree

Kenneth Slessor Selected Poems

Ralph Stow The Merry-Go-Round in the Sea To the Islands

Patrick White The Tree of Man

David Williamson The Removalists